SEVENTY YE

AT HAMMONDS FARM

1735 - 1804

DUNCAN ROBERTSON

2024

Copyright © Duncan Robertson, 2024

All rights reserved by the author.

No part of this publication may be reproduced or transmitted in any form by any means without the consent of the author.

With the consent of the author, this edition has been published by Mel Thompson on behalf of the Little Baddow History Centre.

For Madeleine and my family

To those who think I struggle
with the law. The 18th century
was not easy.

To Nick with thanks for all your help
Duncan

Acknowledgements

Thank you to the estate of Sheila Rowley, Jill Goodson, John Bundock, Jim Leaver and Mel Thompson for the valuable information their books have given me. Colleen Devenish and John Barrett have been a great help with the historical presentation. I in particular thank Mel for being my mentor and editor for this project. The University of Nottingham guidance has been extremely useful on the interpretation of documents.

CONTENTS

Preface		6
Introduction		7
1.	1735 Marriage Settlement	17
2.	Who's who for Stoakes and Tagell families	26
3.	1740 Administration and 1742 Mortgage	27
4.	1742 Will of Sarah Tagell	29
5.	1743 William Tagell case	33
6.	1745 Assignment of mortgage and guarantee	36
7.	1746 Declaration of Secret Trust	38
8.	1760s History of Tagell, Sadd and Keys families	40
9.	1762 and 1764 court orders and deed	42
10.	1765 Assignment of mortgage	45
11.	1766 Mortgage	48
12.	1773 Plan explanation	50
13.	1774 Deed of ratification and confirmation of mortgage	51
14.	Who's who in William Hart's family	53
15.	1781 Four deeds	54
16.	1795 Will of William Hart the Elder	58
17.	1798 Will of Samuel Hart	61
18.	1804 Assignment of lease	64
19.	1804 Lease and Release	68
20.	Legal Notes	71
Index of people		79

PREFACE

There are legal notes at the end of this report before the index. For cross reference when I think it is useful I have added 'LN' and the Heading from the legal notes. This report has the punctuation or lack of it favoured by lawyers.

In 1735 we are still in an era when girls could marry at 12 and boys at 14. A married woman's property rights were largely merged with her husband who ruled the roost. Eldest sons were still given priority. It is a bonus that the deeds and documents for my review are in an old form of English and not in Latin as they were prior to 1733. Being a retired lawyer I have reservations that in those days lawyers were paid by the word or the line. This of course resulted in some long rambling documents. This report relates to rare documents of Freehold titles in Little Baddow.

I anticipate that all the original deeds and documents covered by this review will be lodged with Essex Record Office (ERO) for safe keeping. I think it is likely they will put them all in one accession box. Little Baddow History Centre will give guidance as to accessing these records. There are already a number of documents in ERO Accession Box A13186. These include a deed prior to the marriage settlement of 1735, the will of Sarah Tagell of 1742, a barristers advice of 1743 and a deed of 1762. Where possible I will give other ERO references.

INTRODUCTION

Some of the comments in this introduction apply to the properties in Maldon and Bradwell on Sea as well as Hammonds Farm and the Priests Lands . I consider the best way of introducing this report is to consider all the relevant plans relating to the two farms.

PLANS

1. Firstly we have the 1773 plan of Hammonds Farm supplied by Essex Record Office (ERO) Reference D/DQ 54/1 which is my main map source of information. This has been adapted by me into PLAN ONE covering both Hammonds Farm and the Priests Lands and three plans showing the different areas A, B & C. I have incorporated in the A , B & C adaptions the 1839 tithe map numbers in red. I have also added field names in red as provided by Little Baddow History Centre plans dated 1839 and 1843. The tithe records give sizes for nearly all the fields. These are given in Acres, Roods and Perches. Considering PLAN TWO for Area A and the field nearest Hurrells Lane. Firstly 383 is the Tithe field number. The name of the field is Six Acres Prisland. 7/1/16 means 7 acres 1 rood and 16 perches. Just to remind us, there are 4 roods to the acre and 40 perches to the rood. Two acres is about the size of a football pitch. One rood is the size of a tennis court. PLAN TWO covers area A, PLAN THREE covers area B and PLAN FOUR overs area C. PLAN ONE shows that part of Area D comprising about 3 acres is some 340 Metres west of Area C and adjoins what I think was the original route of the River Chelmer. The rest of area D comprising some of the allotment land is close by. These two areas are called Lang Mead.

2. I am not able to identify the exact location of Area E, Broad Mead from the 1773 plan or on the tithe map of 1839 which is PLAN FIVE attached. The 1839 plan shows the route of the canal but not the original river. An extract of the History Centre 1843 map is attached PLAN SIX which shows areas called Land Mead Field and Lang Mead Field. The position of these areas partly tallies with area D on PLAN ONE. I also show on PLAN SIX what I think is the old course of the River Chelmer. The old course of the river is more clearly shown on PLAN SEVEN. What was Hammonds Lane is now called Hammonds Road. The two allotments comprising Area E are somewhere to the north/ west towards Whitwells Farm as shown on the 1839 tithe map. They are some 800 metres to the north/west of the Further Five Acres field in area C. As already mentioned I am not able to locate them precisely.

3. The areas of roads and river are incorporated in the 1773 measurements for the total size of the farms. The roads comprise at least 3 acres. They are no doubt shown as part of the ownership as presumably there was a liability to repair and maintain them. I assume half the width of the river is shown as that has fishing and possibly other rights. May be they used rushes for thatch or harvested watercress? Meadow land boundaries were marked out with posts not fences. This makes location more difficult to establish.

4. There is an extract from the 1777 Chapman and Andre plan of Little Baddow PLAN SEVEN attached that clearly shows the position of the farms in relation to the property Waterhall and the Sandon Brook. Waterhall was also known as Belmours, Belmores, Belmers, Belmirs, Belmarsh and Walters Hall. I do not know the dates for the various name changes although Waterhall was used as the name for this property from the 1800s. Because of all the name changes throughout this report I call that property Waterhall. The plan also shows the position of the Hammonds Farmhouse but does not name it.

PLAN ONE

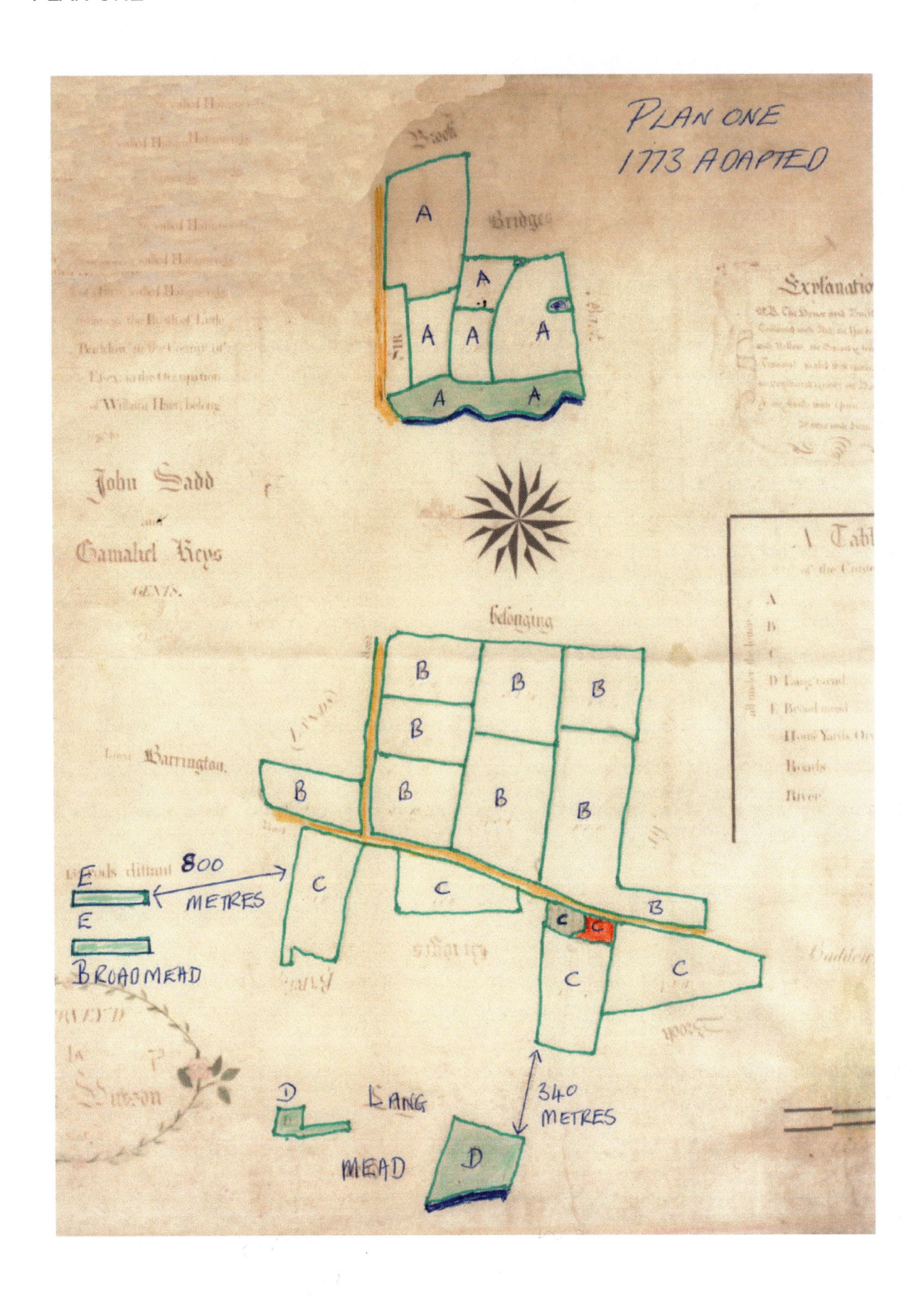

PLAN TWO

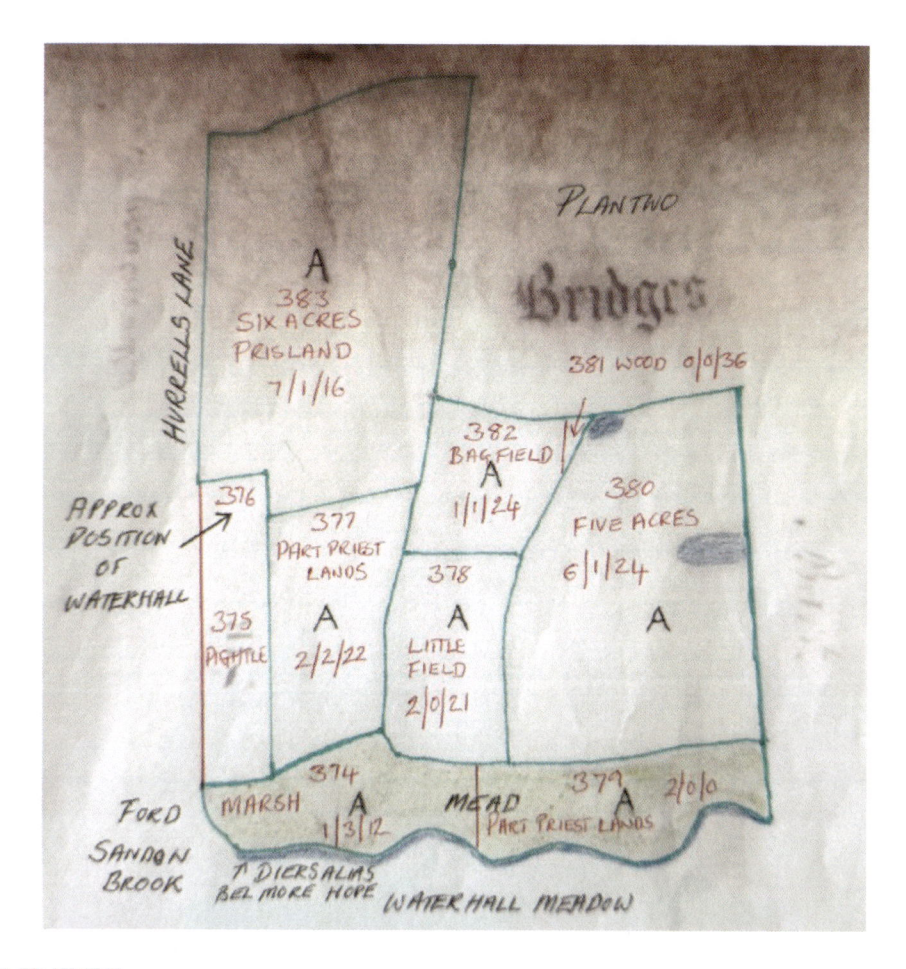

PLAN THREE

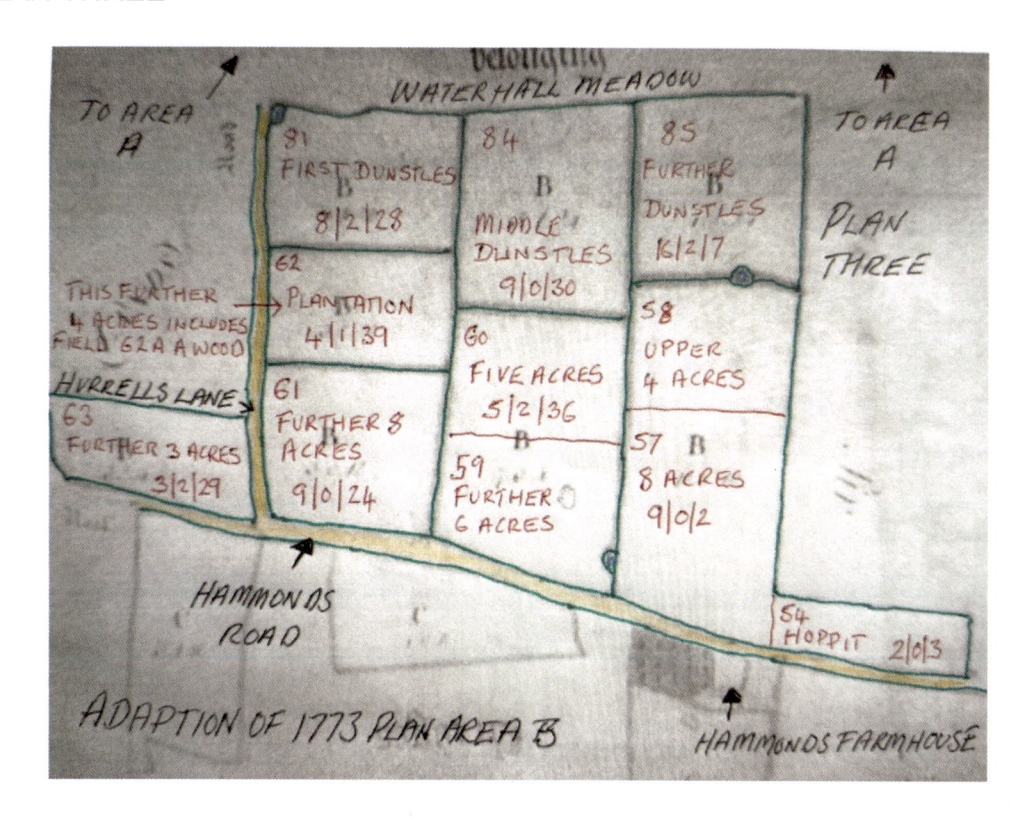

PLAN FOUR

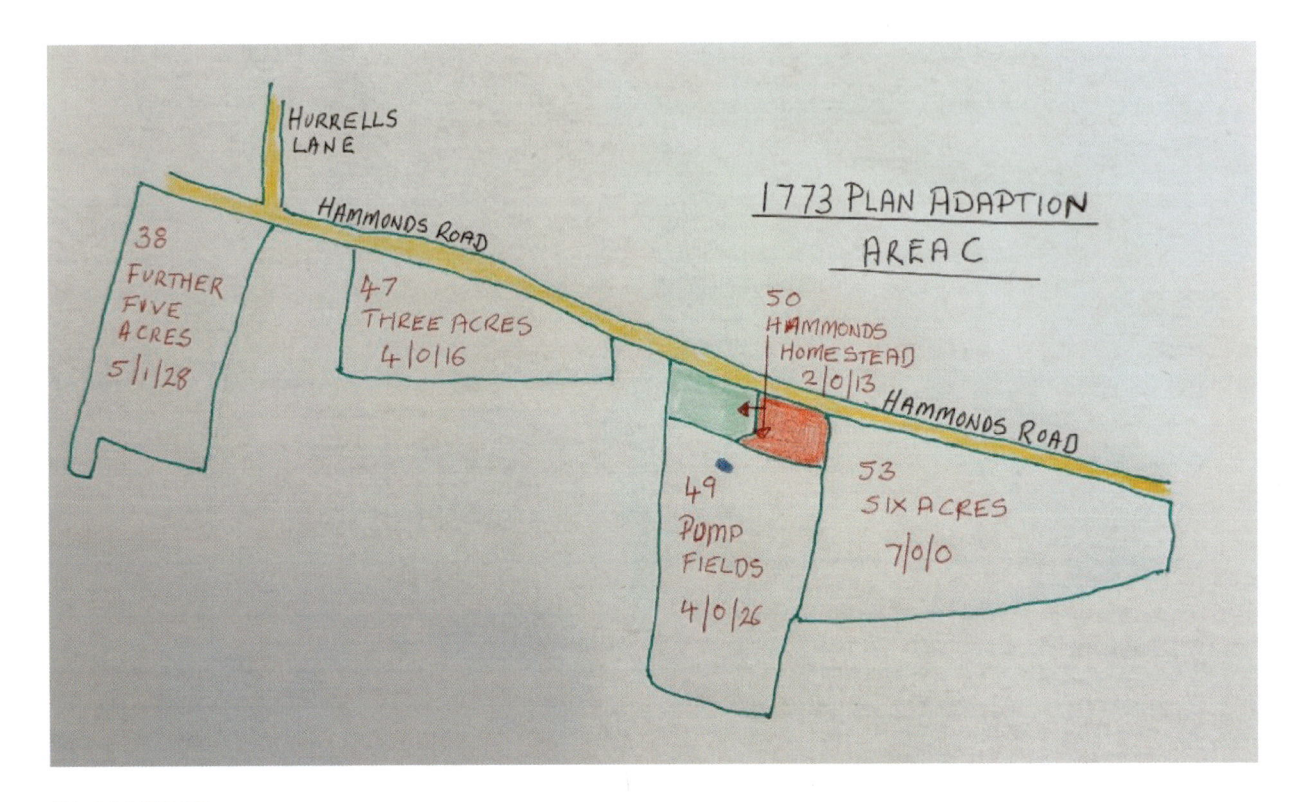

PLAN FIVE

PLAN SIX

PLAN SEVEN

HISTORY OF THE FARMS

The total area of the land referred to in this report extends to about 100 ACRES

1. This is an introduction to the deeds and documents relating to HAMMONDS FARM (75 ACRES) and the PRIESTS LANDS (24 ACRES). Combined they were for a period called TAGELLS FARM. Sometimes together I just call them Hammonds or farms. Hammonds was sometimes spelt Hamonds. Mel Thompson refers to John Balsham selling land to John Hammond in 1385. The tithe records show there was an Edmund Hamonde in occupation in 1399. The farm is using that surname. The name should not be confused with the house now called Pattentees up on The Ridge built in 1694 by a Thomas Hammond. That house was called Hammonds until 1813.

2. Most historians have referred to Hammonds Farm as one with Saxon origins like many farms along the River Chelmer. An interesting point because most of the farm in 1735 is some distance from the river. Only a small area of land probably adjoins the river at that time. I start this history in Saxon Times. Then the River Chelmer had a substantial flood plain as reference to various Meads or Meadows illustrates. Flooding also occurred along the line of the Sandon Brook. I think the Saxon Farms in this area were not aligned with the river but with a track that led from the boundary with Danbury/Sandon northwards along what is now Hammonds Road. The conventional argument would be that the track progressed from Hammonds Road into Church Road to the river. I think we should consider the possibility that the track left Hammonds Road and led up to and past Little Baddow Hall. From the hall there is a very straight footpath round the west end of the St Mary's Church leading down to the river that could have been the line of the track. The track may have led to the Saxon Watermill. The River Chelmer and Sandon Brook will have provided essential water supply for all the farms along the route of the track. To the west of the river beyond the flood plain is the Roman Road to Colchester. Mel Thompson has Roman remains at Waterhall so the history of these farms may go back to those days.

3. In Saxon times there were two manors in Little Baddow. Little Baddow Manor part of the Chelmsford Hundred and Middlemead Manor part of the Dengie (Maldon) Hundred. The farms are in what was the original Little Baddow Hall Manor. From this manor there was devolved a lesser manor of Graces and perhaps a lesser manor of Riffhams. It is Graces that is important for this report. Jim Leaver in his book on Riffhams, states that Riffhams before 1066 was a manor in itself but most other local historians consider it devolved from Little Baddow Manor. He also refers to Riffhams having a mill. I think it was probably for the use of its own Manor and not generally. I prefer to think my Saxon farmers going along the track I describe to that new high-tech water mill that had been built on the River Chelmer. My report does not directly involve Riffhams Manor and the balance of Little Baddow Manor as all the land in this report is in Graces Manor. To add to the confusion on Manors the house and garden at Waterhall were usually regarded as part of Little Baddow Manor. The house at Graces is sometimes shown as being in the Parish of Danbury and part of a manor in that village.

4. We now progress to 1086 and the Little Domesday for Essex, Suffolk and Norfolk that becomes part of the Domesday Book. You could debate for hours what size a Hide was in those days. I am going for a middle figure of 125 acres. I have come to the conclusion that Little Baddow Manor was then about 780 acres. 500 acres were under the direct control of Germond of Oakley as Lord of the Manor. Presumably he had those fields nearest Little Baddow Hall which was the manor house. The other 280 acres were controlled by four unnamed French Men. These would then be the fields further away from the manor house such as those comprising Hammonds Farm and the Priest Lands. The four Norman French Men may have farmed in partnership to start off with but at some stage the land was divided to form individual farms. Being Norman Freemen they would have held the land on a Freehold basis. I think that Hammonds Farm and the Priest Lands have had Freehold titles since that time. (LN on Freeholds). The whole of England was only valued at £73,000 in 1086. Who is going to tell Germond of Oakley if his family hang onto his land for a thousand years he may be able to sell it for £750 million and have 5000 houses built on it?

5. The original name for Priests Lands was Prisland and then Priestlands. Sometimes they are just called Priest Lands. There is no definite evidence of the origin of the name Prislands but in MIddle English 'pris' meant something of great worth. Later it meant price or prize. Perhaps the land was acquired as the result of gambling? I think there is a better explanation. There is evidence that in 1356 John Herward parted with 6 acres to two clergymen (priests) which explains the name that was adopted by the whole farm. Interestingly on the 1839 tithe map the six acre field to the east of Waterhall was called by the old name of Prisland. Sheila Rowley's map of the Manor of Graces shows six fields with the names Prisland that correspond with the 1773 plan. The Priests Lands in 1735 and onwards did not have its own farmhouse. When Waterhall and the Priest Lands were all part of one farm, Waterhall was no doubt the farmhouse. There seems to have been a farmhouse there since at least the 1300s. In 1491 a John Bocher held the freehold comprising 20 acres with 2 acres of meadow. He was paying a nominal 4 shillings a year freehold rent. Because of the nominal rent this looks like part of the freehold land originally owned by one of the Four French Men. By 1614 Sir Henry Mildmay bought Waterhall and the cottage know as Diers alias Belmore Hope from Richard Glascocke. He incorporated them in Graces Manor although Sir Francis Barrington the 1st Baronet still thought the house and garden at Waterhall were in the manor of Little Baddow Hall as does the Barrington Map of 1677. When Sir Henry Milmay dies in 1637 he has Henry Penninge as a tenant farming 18 acres. By the mid 1600s there is a survey that gives the farm as 24 acres with a John Smith occupier of the Waterhall farmhouse as Colonel Mildmay's Tenant. A later note on the survey gives Matthew Rudd as tenant paying £10 a year.

It is clear that Area A on the 1773 Plan is the Priests Lands. The index to the plan gives Area A as nearly 24 acres. None of the green coloured mead land in Area A on the 1773 plan seems to have been subject to any common rights. The tithe map supports the description of the Priests Lands. Field 376 is the house Waterhall. Field 377 is over 2 acres of Priests Lands. Field 379 is 2 acres of Priests Lands being part of the mead to the east of Sandon Brook. Field 383 is the six acre field called by the old name of Prisland.

6. In 1735 there were 8 acres of Common Meadows as part of Hammonds Farm. I think about 5 acres of these are Waterhall Meadows now under the control of Essex Wildlife Trust. These are fields 86 and 87 on the 1839 tithe map. Another 1 acre I suggest is the nursery shown as field 82 on the 1839 tithe map. This nursery replaces the cottage called Diers alias Belmore Hope. The other 2 acres could be a woodland adjoining the meadow land. It might be the mead to the east of the brook but this is unlikely because it would then be in the Priests Lands. In 1839 Waterhall Meadows is pasture land being farmed by Jeremiah Pledger. The fields are then called Long Mead and Slipe. I think this land is Brook Mead and Long Mead as referred to in the 1735 description. There were several fields called Long Mead in Little Baddow. After 1735 the land seems to have lost its common purpose during the next 100 years. If you walk to the end of the Waterhall Meadows there is a clear view across the fields comprising area B on my adaption of the 1773 plan looking towards the Hammonds Farm buildings.

ERO say in their notes with the 1773 plan that the farms include 4 doles which today we would refer to as allotments. These I think are Area E and part of Area D on the adapted plan. Perhaps these small areas provided allotments for the farm workers.

Areas D and E combined on the adapted plan are not big enough to make up the 8 Acres of common land referred to in 1735.

7. As regards Hammonds Farm itself Mel Thompson tells me the farmhouse was moated. He does not know when this was done or for what purpose. It may mean the house was more significant than with other farm houses or it could have been the moat was just a feature. In 1546 there was a survey commission by Sir Thomas Darcy Lord of Graces. It refers to the freehold of Hammonds being held by Robert Grene at rent of 12s a year. That is a nominal rent compatible with him holding the Freehold. The Freehold seems to be held by that family for about 100 years. Sheila Rowley has a farm called Hamonds (held from Graces) occupied by John Walker paying a yearly rent of £34.13.4

presumably as tenant of the Grene family. She refers to the arable, pasture and meadow land lying 'almost surrounded with the land of Colonel Henry Mildmay' amounting to 63 acres. She gives field names including Kitchine Croft, Home Pytell, Doppers, Nerogate Field and Hawkins Piece. Her map however identifies the field called Dunstall and the two meads one of which is called Longmead. The History Centre plans and the tithe plan have names but not the same as given by Sheila Rowley in her description of field names. This is part of the area marked B, C, D & E on the 1773 plan. The 1773 plan indicates that the farm was virtually surrounded by land owned by Sir Brook Bridges the successor to the Mildmay Family. Part of the farms in 1773 adjoins land owned by the Barrington Family.

8. Francis Perkins bought Hammonds Farm and the Priest Lands in 1690 and farmed them together. He was a man of some substance and in 1715 decided to sell his estates in Essex. On the 1st October 1715 he transferred these estates to trustees Lord Stawell and Richard Baggott. He was trying to bar an entail (LN on Entailment) that existed and prevent his wife Annabella claiming any Dower on his death. (LN on Wills and Inheritance). The papers refer to the Priest Lands comprising 22 acres occupied by John Jefferies. Hammonds Farm is referred to as having 57 acres and 6 acres of Meadow. There was another 8 acres close to Graces and Hammonds in a separate set of deeds. On the 3rd December 1717 all of the Graces Estate was sold to Robert Clerke except for the Priest Lands and Hammonds Farm. Some time between 1717 and 1735 Widow Sarah Stoakes acquire the freehold of the two farms but there is no evidence as to when the title passed to her. This is the start of her being a bit of a mystery woman of Little Baddow.

9. In Area B there is an issue about field sizes in 1839 compared with 1773. In particular the fields First Dunstles, Middle Dunstles and Further Dunstles are much bigger in 1839. There may have been woodland that was part of the common land between Waterhall Meadow and these three fields which was cut down to increase the size of the fields. On PLAN TWO the tithe field 375 is called Pighte which means a small enclosure often hedged. I think it was garden and orchard for the house Waterhall.

GENERAL OBSERVATIONS

1. We have with both farms what is best described as a conventional Freehold title rather than a customary title like a Copyhold. Researching manorial records is going to reveal very little. We have a Freehold title for both farms that has existed since the Norman Conquest. Transfer transactions involving both farms were mainly dealt with by a lease and release procedure (LN on Lease and Release) with conventional rather than customary tenancies. One of the main purposes of the lease and release procedure was the fact you did not have to enrol the details. We are in an era where secrecy was part of the culture if not an obsession. Not like today where everybody can find the details of property transactions by searching with the Land Registry.

2. A lot of the deeds I will be examining have nominal considerations shown. Nobody now has any idea of the real money that was passing hands. Although conventional Freehold titles were used a lot nationally those of our Four Frenchmen could be novel for Little Baddow. My investigation of titles in the village such as those deriving out of the Holybread Farm Estate and the Estate that comprised in part Joyces Farm indicate that customary copyhold titles were common in Little Baddow.

3. A common issue involving a lot of the papers for review is the fact Married Women could not control land in their own name. This social injustice was not resolved until 1882. We start in 1735 with a marriage settlement for Sarah Wolvett who married William Tagell. The farms with other property after she died were inherited by her two daughters Hannah and Sarah. How different the deeds would be if these ladies owned the property outright in their own names. Perhaps as both had the maiden name Tagell they may still have used that name for the combined farm. The mortgage arrangements for the farms involve the Fowler family at Graces. Fanny Fowler as a child was the heiress of Graces and large parts of Little Baddow and Danbury would have been under her control as a

spinster once she became an adult. This was not the case and in fact there had to be an Act of Parliament in 1765 to enable her as a spinster and minor to convey, assign and settle her real and personal estate on her intended marriage to Sir Brook Bridges Baronet. Fanny Fowler has a connection with Jane Austen that I will deal with later in this report. How different it would have been if the 1773 plan had been able to show Hannah Keys and Sarah Sadd as the owners of the farms and most of the surrounding land owned by Dame Fanny Bridges. Even more interesting would have been Sarah Wolvett and Fanny Fowler not marrying. We would have then had a large part of Little Baddow and Danbury under the control of a couple of spinsters.

4. In 1735 agriculture was probably still the bedrock of the economy. Trade and industry were increasing all the time and would be dominant by 1804. By the first Census in 1801 only about one third of the working population was occupied in agriculture. By the end of 1700s 80/90% of privately owned farm land was occupied on fixed annual payments. Copyhold was becoming a thing of the past although still common in Little Baddow.

5. Land in the 1700s as now was not a uniform commodity. The quality of land was important with arable fields worth substantially more than meadows, pasture and probably woods. Agriculture was a precarious business subject to the vagaries of climate, disease and prices. Even then the farmers were always grumbling. There was no concept of a Property Market as we know today. No estate agents, no auctioneers or other reliable information on values. There was a different culture. Landlords thought it was normal for there being up to 10% rent arrears. This often led to an abatement or remission in rent. Sometimes Landlords would help with repairs even though they were not obliged to do so.

6. Although my report ends in 1804 it is worth mentioning that by the 1850s the Pledger Family were farming locally 860 acres and employing 50 workers in Little Baddow. The current Hammonds Farmhouse was rebuilt about 1825. This was regarded as one of the headquarters of the 'Pledger Empire' along with Holybread Farmhouse. The Pledgers as modern farmers probably had more influence than some of the lords of the manor who were old fashioned farmers relying on pasture, meadows and woods. The Hammonds arm of the Pledger Family at this time appear to be more closely linked to St Mary's and the Church of England rather than the Chapel. They were buried at St Mary's but this might have been a matter of convenience. The Holybread Pledgers have strong links to the Chapel.

FINANCIAL MATTERS

VALUES

1. There is a difficulty in determining the worth of £1 between 1735 and 1804 with the value of the £ today. I have rejected the Bank of England calculator as that only considers inflation. I have considered the Consumer Price Inflation (CPI) calculator using information from the Office of National Statistics. Unfortunately this does not do calculations prior to 1750. There is a measuring worth calculator that gives £1 in 1735 now worth £167 but that may be linked to inflation only. There is other evidence that suggests a figure of £300 for 1735. This fits in with the CPI which gives £284 in 1750, £230 in 1770 and £128 in 1804. There is a variation on this index I have used that gives £278 in 1750, £228 in 1770 and £125 in 1804. No index can be precise. There is no link to price increase due to property or land values. The value of the pound reduces considerably during my period of review. There are a number of national events that could explain the decline. You have the Jacobite Rebellion in 1745. The American Revolution that started in the 1760s and then at the end of my review period the Napoleonic Wars.

2. The average rent needs to be considered. Arthur Young the agricultural writer made a tour of Eastern England in the 1760s and came to the conclusion the average rent was 70p per acre. He then gives an average rent of 76p per acre for Eastern England in

1790. There are some historians who have reservations about him. Most see him as the best source of information. There is another writer called H G Hunt who gives an average rent in 1800 of 75p per acre for South East England. After 1800 rents shot up so that by 1820 they were £1 per acre. This despite some bad harvests and a lot of farms going out of business. You need to be careful about considering rents for Copyhold compared with Freeholds having conventional tenancies. Copyhold rent could be substantially less for a variety of reasons. Rental values were important for tax calculations.

3. When considering comparable land values I would ignore prices paid for manors. They usually involved a valuable manor house. They often had a substantial hope value where there was common land with enclosure potential. Enclosure led to the privatisation of land. I do not discuss enclosure in any great detail as it is not particularly relevant to our two farms. There was about 8 acres of common land lost from Hammonds Farm.

4. Land in 1700s was regarded as a low risk investment. Many like they do today thought it had a greater return than just the flow of rental income that then yielded about 2%.

TAX AND TITHE

1. There was in the 1700s despite Land Tax a taxation switch from land to consumption that would have impacted on values. There was excise duty on things like salt and candles as well as wine and beer.

2. We have taxes such as those on hearths and windows and these would have impact so far as the Hammonds Farmhouse is concerned. There is evidence of the bricking up of windows to mitigate that tax. These would also have applied to the houses in Maldon and Bradwell on Sea.

3. Land Tax was introduced in 1692 and would have a major impact on the farms. It was charged each year to the owners of the land taking into account the size of the holding and its rental value.

4. Tax on death and inheritance was another issue. Between Magna Carta and 1974 when Inheritance Tax in its current form was introduced there were 12 different death taxes introduced. Many of these were from the late 1600s to 1800 to fund wars. Certainly deaths due to Black Death and Plague generated a lot of extra tax.

5. Tithe was payable on both farms between 1735 and 1804. This involved a tenth of the produce of land and stock paid by landholders to the church. Sometimes the right to collect tithes passed into lay hands. This was not abolished until 1836 when they substituted rent charges. The tithe on the farms fluctuated with the average value of the crop or stock. Tithe was often paid by the tenant and then deducted from rent. It was shared between the vicar and rector according to custom.

Some of what follows other than the legal notes is 'History according to Duncan'. There is some speculation where I am uncertain of the facts.

1

1735 MARRIAGE SETTLEMENT

The first document for review and report is a marriage settlement dated 6th March 1735 relating to the marriage of Mr William Tagell of Maldon to Miss Sarah Wolvett of Little Baddow. The settlors (the people making the settlement) are Sarah Stoakes widow of Little Baddow grandmother of Sarah Wolvett and John Tagell with his wife Hannah of Maldon the father and mother of William Tagell.

THE PEOPLE INVOLVED

1. Sarah Stoakes (sometimes spelt Stokes) widow of Little Baddow has had two husbands Mr Wolvett followed by Mr Stoakes. In 1735 she owns the freehold of Hammonds Farm, the Priests Lands and various common meadows in Little Baddow. She also owns various freehold properties at Bradwell on Sea. Going to the end of the deed she has a very interesting mark. Not just your usual X. She was a comparatively rich widow who appears to be illiterate. Sheila Rowley in her books refers to Widow Stokes being Overseer of the Poor in 1733. People like Lord Barrington have fulfilled this role so it seems it was a bit of an honour to have this appointment. Sheila Rowley mentions Widow Stokes because she is one of very few women who had their work as overseer undertaken by a man on her behalf. This is understandable if she was illiterate. In 1735 it was a real benefit being able to read and write. There was a great social stigma being middle class and illiterate. Sarah Stokes must have had considerable social status to be Overseer of the Poor. She was in charge of the Poor House and a budget of £60 pa. This is equivalent to £18,000 today. Benefits then were a lot different than they are today. As well as shelter the poor only needed food, clothes and help to get out of their predicament. No mobile phone contracts to pay then.

The first question is where in Little Baddow were her and her granddaughter living. I doubt if any of the grander houses was available. I do not think this was Hammonds Farm because at that time despite it may be having a moat it would have been fairly basic accommodation. I think Robert Martin her tenant occupied it. The improved house at Hammonds was not built until the 1820s. I think they lived at Waterhall a substantial Hall House. A suitable house for a wealthy widow. The land called Priests Lands adjoins Waterhall and seems to have been conveyed separately from that property sometime prior to 1735. Priests Lands in 1735 comprised 24 acres. I am not sure if Sarah Stoakes owned Waterhall or was she renting it from the Mildmay Family?

The second question is how did Sarah Stoakes acquire such a large estate of property. There is some evidence of inheritance in particular as to the Bradwell on Sea properties.

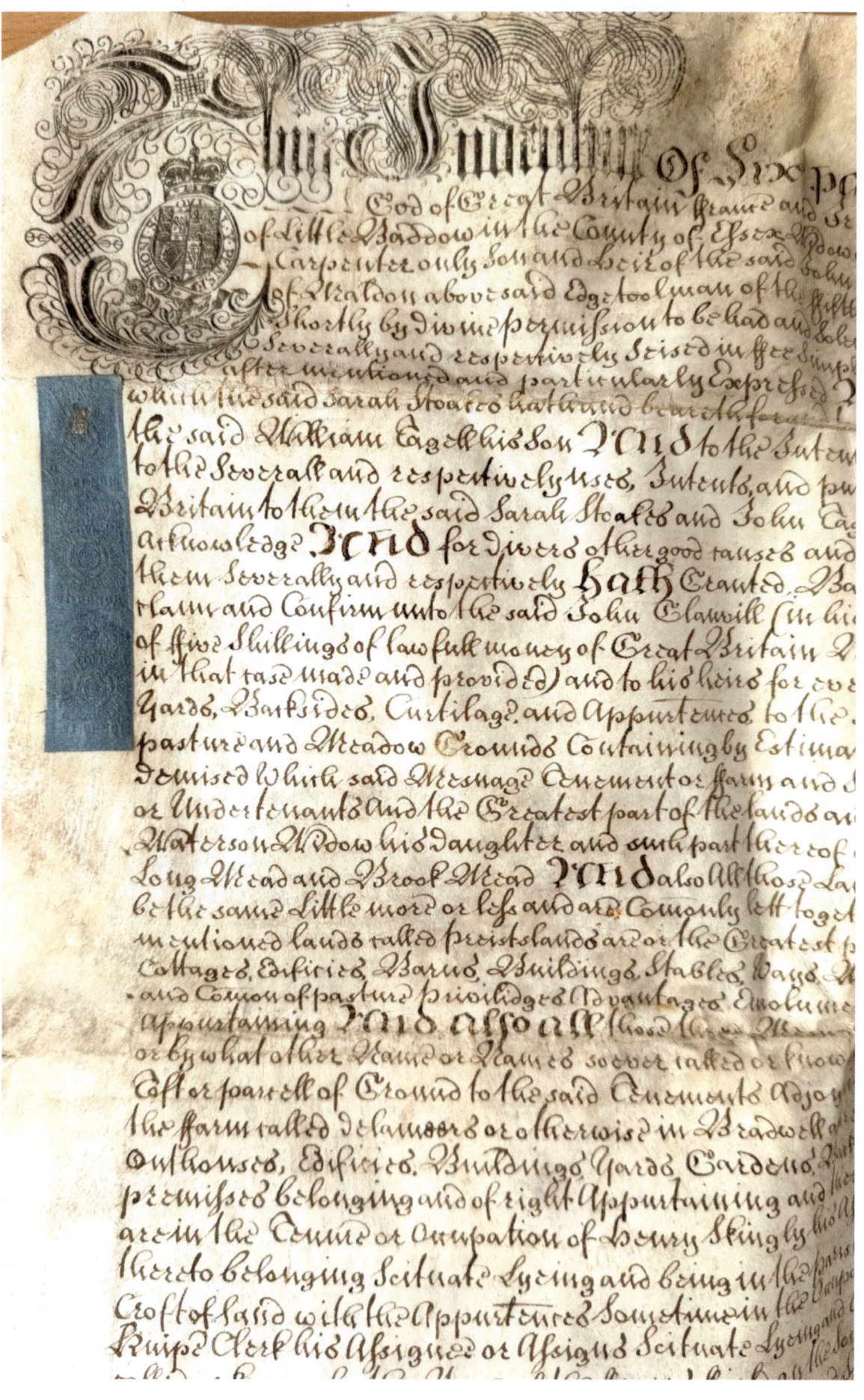

An extract from the 1735 Marriage Settlement.

These may have been owned by her parents. One assumes as she is a widow some property could have been inherited from her late husbands. She may have been entitled to a Dower. (LN Wills and Inheritance). Her ownership might have been as a result of a family settlement. Her two estates may have come from different sources.

2. Sarah Wolvett is a spinster living in Little Baddow presumably with her grand mother. The deed indicates that Sarah Stoakes had more than one son but there is no mention of daughters. Her father is George Wolvett and I presume his wife, her mother has died. George Wolvett is the eldest son by Sarah Stoakes first marriage which we find out later in this report. Benjamin Stoakes is the eldest son of the second marriage. George Wolvett is very much the black sheep of the family and has disappeared. Sarah Stoakes does not acknowledge him as her son in the deed. There is a contingency provision for George Wolvett. If Sarah Wolvett and William her husband to be both die without children George then if he reappears receives £25 (£7,500 today) pa for life. There is no provision for Sarah Stoakes having daughters or any other grandchild except Sarah Wolvett. It seems her grandmother brought her up from an early age after her mother died. This is a time when married women have limited property rights. The only effective way of protecting the position of Sarah Wolvett is by way of this marriage settlement. I am not sure of her age when she married but assume she was in her late teens or early twenties. She and William married at St Mary's Church Little Baddow on the 8th March 1735. The marriage records give various spellings of her surname, Woolvch, Woolvet and Woolvit. She signs the deed with a cross so is also illiterate.

3. John Tagell of Maldon and his wife Hannah both sign the end of the deed and therefore one assumes they are literate. There is evidence later in this report that Hannah lived to a good age and may have been illiterate. Perhaps she had some assistance in signing the deed to avoid the middle class stigma of being illiterate. Although the deed describes John Tagell as a Coal Meeter there is evidence that he was a master carpenter by trade. Although at this time there was only limited shipbuilding in Maldon there would have been a lot of ship repair work to keep a carpenter busy. In the early 1700s coal was one of the major imports into Maldon. By the 1700s coal was becoming the main source of energy taking over from woodburning. It was mined in the north of England and brought to Maldon by boat. There were at this time over 1,200 collier ships taking ' Sea Coal ' out of Newcastle with a substantial number going to Maldon. You definitely at that time would not be taking coals to Newcastle. You can imagine that if John Tagell is heavily involved in the import of coal into Maldon it has made him a wealthy man. Maldon was one of the largest coal ports due to difficulties in navigating the Thames. There is evidence of pack horse routes leading from Maldon one of which came through Little Baddow. Based on tonnage Mel Thompson estimates that 80 packhorses a day passed through our village. This was in addition to the wagons going over Danbury Hill.

We need to understand the role of John Tagell as a Coal Meeter or Meter. This was an appointment created by Act of Parliament. He superintends the measurement of coal when it leaves the ship and goes into sacks. Originally it was by volume but later the measurement was by weight. If the measurement was by volume he had to make sure the sacks were well filled. A lot of regulation was by way of local custom. Unloading at speed was important. You needed a man trusted by the ship owners and the first buyers. He took commission from both buyer and seller which no doubt is what made him wealthy.

4. William Tagell of Maldon is a carpenter and the only son and heir of John Tagell. He became an apprentice in 1724 and his father paid a premium of £15 (£4,500 today) to James Ougham for his training. I remember in the 1960s parents were still paying a premium for training in some professions. I imagine in 1724 he was about 15 which would make him 26 when he got married. As a master carpenter he took on an apprentice himself in 1737. This was John Peers of Tarling (aka Terling). His father John an Inn Holder paid a premium of £12 (£3,600 today). It would be nice to think that as a carpenter he went to work at Waterhall and fell in love with Sarah Wolvett. Sadly I doubt if this is the case as the deed implies that the settlement is made on the basis of the marriage being arranged. If Sarah Stoakes could not find an eligible bachelor in Little Baddow for her granddaughter then Maldon would be a logical place to look. As he is the

only son and heir then presumably he will inherit the carpentry business but not the job of Coal Meter.

5. John Glanville of Maldon Esq and toolman. Later in the papers it says that he is an Edge Toolman. This was a specialist blacksmith hardening and tempering blades. Normally the specialism was for making agricultural tools but it could be for mining tools. Tools for cutting coal in Maldon would be very useful. The reference to Esquire is the important factor here. John signs the deed so is literate. He is the lead of two trustees and has the freeholds of all the settled land vested in him. He has to be a person who all the other parties to this settlement trust completely. Esquire in this case indicates that John Glanville was something like a justice of the peace and of some considerable social standing. John Tagell was no doubt a friend. They seem to have a similar social status.

6. William Barker yeoman of Fairstead in Essex is the second trustee and his role is very much to protect the interests of the family of Sarah Stoakes. The term yeoman is difficult to define and in 1735 would be someone regarded as not quite gentry. There would be many farmers self sufficient but old fashioned who would like to be called yeoman. In this case the term would appear to be justified. The Essex Archives say that William Barker Yeoman was involved with a lease in Thaxted in 1737. He seems to have property interests in other parts of the county. The deed is in six identical parts and this is only one copy. There is a seal affixed to the end of this part of the deed but it does not look as if William Barker has signed it. I have no explanation for this omission other than this may be the part that William Barker was to keep.

THE PROPERTIES AND LAND INVOLVED

LITTLE BADDOW

1. There are three different areas of land all of which are occupied by Robert Martin as tenant of Sarah Stoakes. He in turn has various undertenants. There is a full description of the property in the deed including the messuage, cottages, barns and other features such as woods, timber and trees.

2. The first area of land is Hammonds Farm comprising 70 acres. It has a farmhouse which presumably is occupied by Robert Martin.

Hammonds farmhouse as it has been since the 1820s.

An old barn next to Hammonds Farmhouse that could have existed in the 1700s.

3. The second area of land that is part of the 70 acres is common meadows comprising 8 acres. There are two meadows one called Long Mead and the other Brook Mead. I think that part of this land is Waterhall Meadow. If these Meads were both down towards and adjoining the river they would have comprised a larger area than referred to on the 1773 plan. The word Brook however indicates that it is an area adjoining Sandon Brook. It could be the mead to the east of Sandon Brook but that land is in the Priest Lands Farm rather than Hammonds Farm. I do not think we can be certain as to where the common meadows are situate. Reference is made to common pasture privileges so presumably there were common grazing rights exercised by others in the community over this land.

Waterhall as it is today.

4. Thirdly we have the 24 acres of Priests Lands which is part of the land comprising the original Waterhall Farm minus the house garden and orchard now comprised in a separate title occupied by Sarah Stoakes and her Granddaughter Sarah Wolvett.

5. There is reference to all of the Little Baddow land being surrounded by the lands of the late Colonel Henry Mildmay and now Elizabeth Waterson, widow his daughter. She features again in this report as she is aunt of Edmund Fowler and leaves the Graces Estate to him.

BRADWELL ON SEA

Ramble House, 9 High Street, Bradwell on Sea, as it is today.

6. The properties in Bradwell on Sea were also owned by Sarah Stoakes. There is a fold and hole in the parchment of the deed which makes this part of the document difficult to read. There is reference to two houses called Great Lords and Little Lords. There is much confusion as the spelling of names. These were a pair of late medieval two-cell houses called Great Leaches and Little Leeches otherwise known as Great Leeds and Little Leeds. They are now Ramble House 9 and Kemble House 11 High Street Bradwell on Sea. They were built in the first half of the 1500s as a pair of two cell semi-detached houses with a continuous front jetty. That means a first floor cantilever jutting out over the ground floor. They are the first pair of this type of house with floored halls to be identified in Essex. There is reference to a third house. There is a croft on which there was formerly a house abutting a farm called Delamoors to the west of the Kings Highway. There is today a Delameres Farm adjoining the Maldon Road near Bradwell Village Hall. These properties are also tenanted.

MALDON

37 Church Street, The Hythe, as it is today.

St Mary's Church, The Hythe, as it is today.

7. The property owned by John Tagell with his wife is a freehold house in the Parish of St Mary's in Maldon occupied by their son William. It has an orchard and there is a separate croft of land that is rented out. I presume the croft is relatively small comprising a few acres. It abuts a field formerly called Millfield and then named Fryers Field. I think this house is intended as the matrimonial home for William and his new bride Sarah. This property is treated differently in the trust arrangements which exclude Sarah Stoakes having any interest in it. St Mary's Church (famed for its beacon to light the way for ships) is near the port area of the Hythe. The Hythe was a hamlet separate from Maldon town. It is odd that the house is not named. There is an unnamed 17th century hall house at 37 Church Street opposite St Mary's Church that could be this property. A good place to live if you are going to inherit a carpenter's business down by the Hythe.

PURPOSE OF SETTLEMENT

1. I am pretty certain that all the property involved is Freehold. John Glanville as the lead trustee has all the property held in his name. The house in Maldon refers to it being freehold and I consider all the other property is also freehold. There are two references to the properties being transferred to John Glanville in fee simple and they being unincumbered. This implies there are no mortgages outstanding and Sarah Stoakes and John Tagell own their respective freehold properties outright.

2. The deed is in six parts presumably with identical wording and cut from the one sheet of parchment. The deed has wavy lines at the top which is common with indentures of many parts where one set of wavy lines should match the other when cut. This looks like the last part to be prepared with a straight line at the end which supports the argument that it is the part for William Barker to keep so there is no need for him to sign it.

3. Now this is where the position becomes more complex. We must remember the lawyers were paid by the word and wanted to cover everything on a belt and braces basis in particular when there is a gift of property is involved. In those days they would have been very mindful of the rule that you are not able to perfect an imperfect gift. All parties have a power to assign their interest.

4. It is clear there is a settled land intention in the deed with the settlors Sarah Stoakes and John Tagell with his wife Hannah transferring because of their natural love and affection for their offspring. Each of them have the benefit of their respective properties until the marriage is finalised.

5. There is 10 shillings paid by John Granville on a bargain and sale basis. On the 5th March he was paid by way of a separate indenture 5s to comply with the law on uses. This was a release under a lease and release procedure (LN Lease and Release). An original part of the deed of release is held by ERO as part of Accession Box A13186. Again it looks like the final part not signed by William Barker. As we will discover later in this report the Lease part of this procedure went missing. I consider this was a belt and braces operation to transfer all estates including the freeholds to John Glanville as trustee. There is an onus on him throughout the deed to 'preserve the contingent estate'.

6. As to the property in Little Baddow Sarah Stoakes retains a life interest and receives all the rent from Robert Martin.

7. When she dies there is a special trust set up under the control of William Barker. This is for a term of 1000 years which was a common length of term for this type of arrangement. This trust secures a payment of £200 to Benjamin Stoakes one of the sons of Sarah Stoakes if he is alive. £200 is about the same as £60,000 today. We find out later he is not very happy with this provision and thinks he is treated unfairly. William Barker may mortgage the property within one year of her death to make this payment. He is entitled to costs and charges for dealing with this facility.

8. In Little Baddow William Tagell has a life interest followed by Sarah his wife and then their children in such proportions as Sarah their mother thinks appropriate. There is a contingency if they do not have children. She may have other children who inherit. For example if William dies she could remarry and have children by her second husband.

9. As previously mentioned if there are no children then William Barker holds for another 99 years to pay whilst he lives George Wolvett the father of Sarah £25 per annum. This is to be paid from the rents of Hammonds Farm and the Priests Lands. The residue will pass with the estate of Sarah his daughter.

10. As to the properties in Bradwell on Sea, Sarah Stoakes retains an interest receiving the rent from those properties until the marriage of her granddaughter on the 8th March.

11. Next it is her granddaughter Sarah who has a life interest as from her marriage which will give her an income completely independent from William her husband. She is entitled to the rent from all of these properties from 8th March 1735 the day she marries This is unusual in a world that favours men most of the time. William has the next life interest followed by such of their children as Sarah their mother thinks appropriate or if none her other children or heirs.

12. As to the property in Maldon John Tagell and his wife Hannah have a joint life interest followed by William their son and then Sarah his wife. This time the next life interest is such of their children as William thinks appropriate or if none his heirs.

13. There are covenants by the settlors confirming their freehold ownership and for further deeds that may be required by John Granville. It also covers costs and fees incurred by him and William Barker.

14. The object of course is for each family to protect their position so far as possible. Having said that the Tagell family seem to do quite well out of this settlement. There is a bias towards the position of the man which was common in the 1700s.

2

Who's who for Stoakes and Tagell families

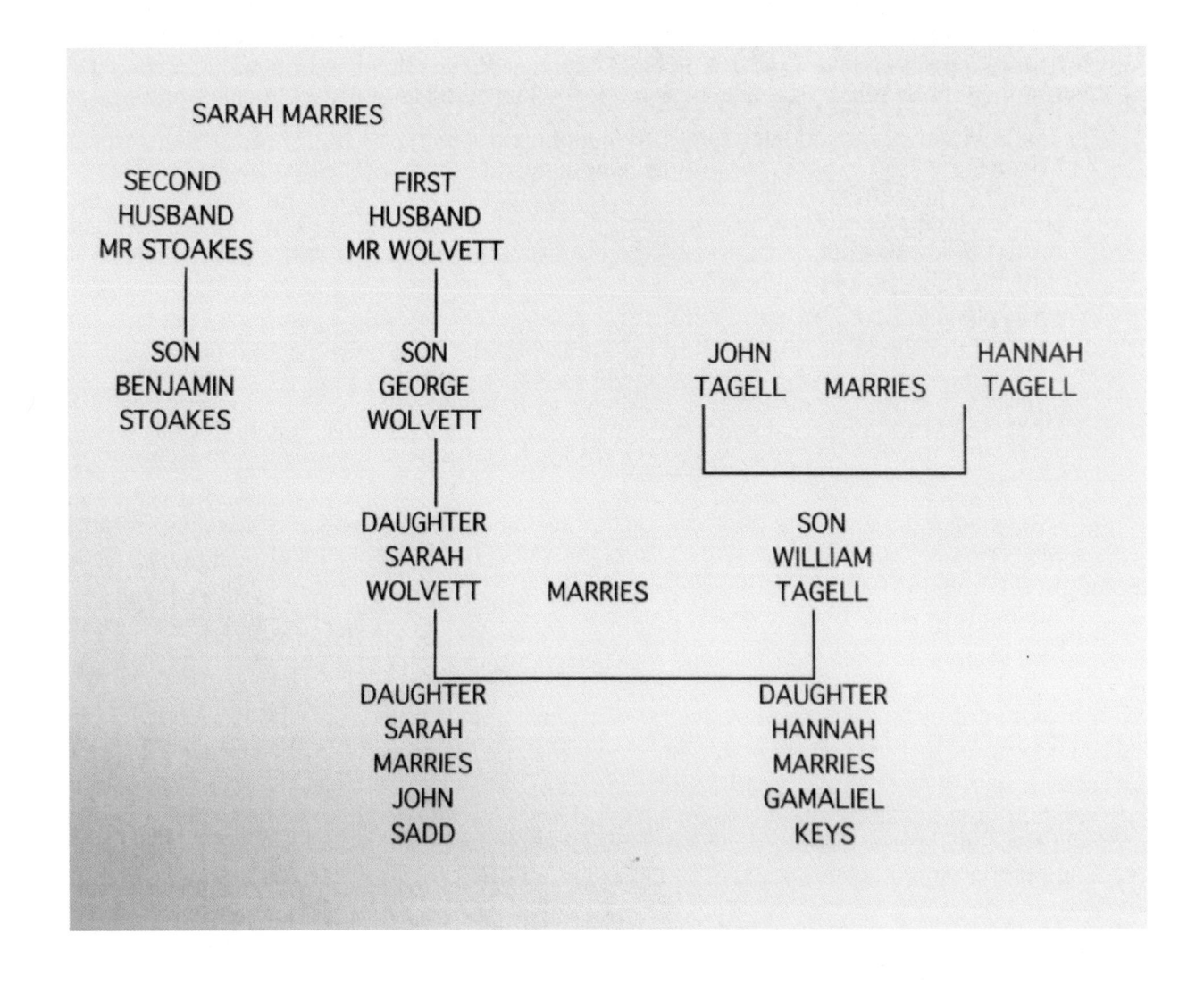

```
                    SARAH MARRIES

      SECOND              FIRST
      HUSBAND             HUSBAND
      MR STOAKES          MR WOLVETT
          |                   |
          |                   |
        SON                 SON              JOHN                    HANNAH
      BENJAMIN            GEORGE            TAGELL    MARRIES        TAGELL
      STOAKES             WOLVETT
                              |                          |
                              |                          |
                          DAUGHTER                     SON
                           SARAH                     WILLIAM
                          WOLVETT     MARRIES        TAGELL
                              |                          |
                              |                          |
                          DAUGHTER                   DAUGHTER
                           SARAH                     HANNAH
                          MARRIES                    MARRIES
                           JOHN                     GAMALIEL
                           SADD                       KEYS
```

26

3

1740 Administration and 1742 Mortgage

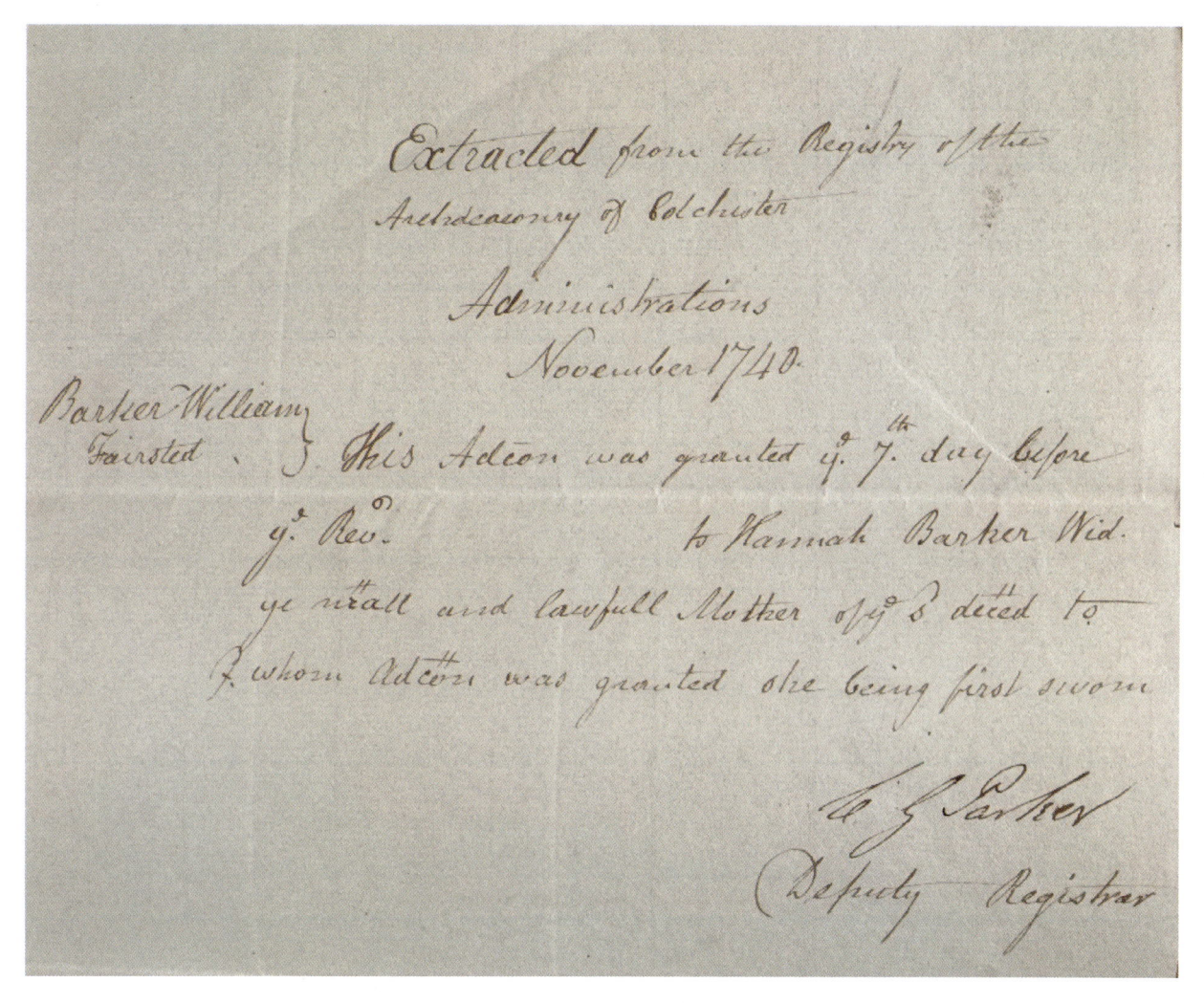

[Handwritten document extract:]

> Extracted from the Registry of the
> Archdeaconry of Colchester
>
> Administrations
> November 1740
>
> Barker William
> Fairsted. This Adcōn was granted ye 7th day before
> ye Revo.   to Hannah Barker Wid.
> ye natrall and lawfull Mother of ye d decd to
> whom Adcōn was granted she being first sworn
>
>   G Parker
>   (Deputy) Registrar

We have an extract from the Register of the Archdeaconry of Colchester dated 7th November 1740 in relation to the estate of William Barker of Fairstead. The administration of his estate was granted to Hannah Barker a widow his lawful mother. We do not have a copy of the Mortgage of the 24th March 1742 but we have details from a subsequent assignment of 1745. Having a full recital of the details of the mortgage is very useful.

THE PEOPLE INVOLVED

1. Sarah Stoakes grandmother of Sarah Wolvett now Tagell has died.

2. William Barker has died. I think he was intestate and did not leave a will.

3. Hannah Barker is the mother of William Barker the second trustee in the 1735 Marriage Settlement. It was his job to protect the interests of the Stoakes Family. She has a lease for 1000 years under the terms of the Marriage Settlement. She is allowed to enter into the mortgage as the administratrix of the estate of her son without any further deed being required. Nowadays you would in these circumstances probably have a deed confirming the position of John Glanville as the lead trustee bearing in mind his obligation to preserve the contingent estate. For some reason he is not a party to the mortgage.

4. Benjamin Stoakes otherwise spelt Stokes is one of the sons of Sarah Stoakes and he is entitled to a payment of £200 (today worth £60,000) under the terms of the Marriage Settlement.

5. William and Sarah Tagell are living in Maldon. They are regarded as the borrowers responsible for repaying the loan.

6. Nicholas Monk of Tarling is the person making the loan. He is a Tanner and his business is in Fairstead the same village where William Barker lived and presumably knew him, his mother and the Stoakes family. There is at that time a Tannery at Fuller Street, Fairstead near Tarling. Because of the size of the loan I presume Nicholas Monk is the owner of that tannery. There seems to be a ready supply of tree bark and plant leaves to create the chemical called tannin to operate the tannery. The tannery will have converted skins and hides into leather. Then the leather workers would have made items such as bridles, shoes and buckets. In those days tanneries were usually substantial businesses.

PROPERTIES

It is only the farms of Hammonds and the Priests Lands that are subject to the mortgage. The properties in Maldon and Bradwell on Sea are not part of this arrangement.

PURPOSES OF THE MORTGAGE

1. Nicholas Monk provides £200 to fund the payment to Benjamin Stoakes on the security of the properties.

2. Under the terms of the 1735 Marriage Settlement a term of 1000 years is vested in Hannah Barker. She receives a nominal 5 shillings.

3. William and Sarah Tagell have agreed to the creation of the mortgage which is by way of lease for a term of 999 years at a peppercorn rent. They are responsible for repaying the loan and interest.

4. Lawful interest is paid on the loan. The maximum at that time was 5% but it may have been slightly less, say 4%.

5. There is a normal right of redemption in this case on the 25th September 1742 (LN Mortgages).

1742 Will of Sarah Tagell

1. We only have a copy of this document the original is held by ERO in Accession Box 13186.
2. The will is dated 31st January 1742 and was therefore made prior to Sarah Tagell joining in the Mortgage of the 24th March .
3. It confirms she is the wife of William Tagell carpenter who I presume has taken over the carpentry business of John Tagell his father who has died.
4. Sarah's Grandmother Sarah Stoakes is dead but we do not know if her father George Wolvett is alive or not.

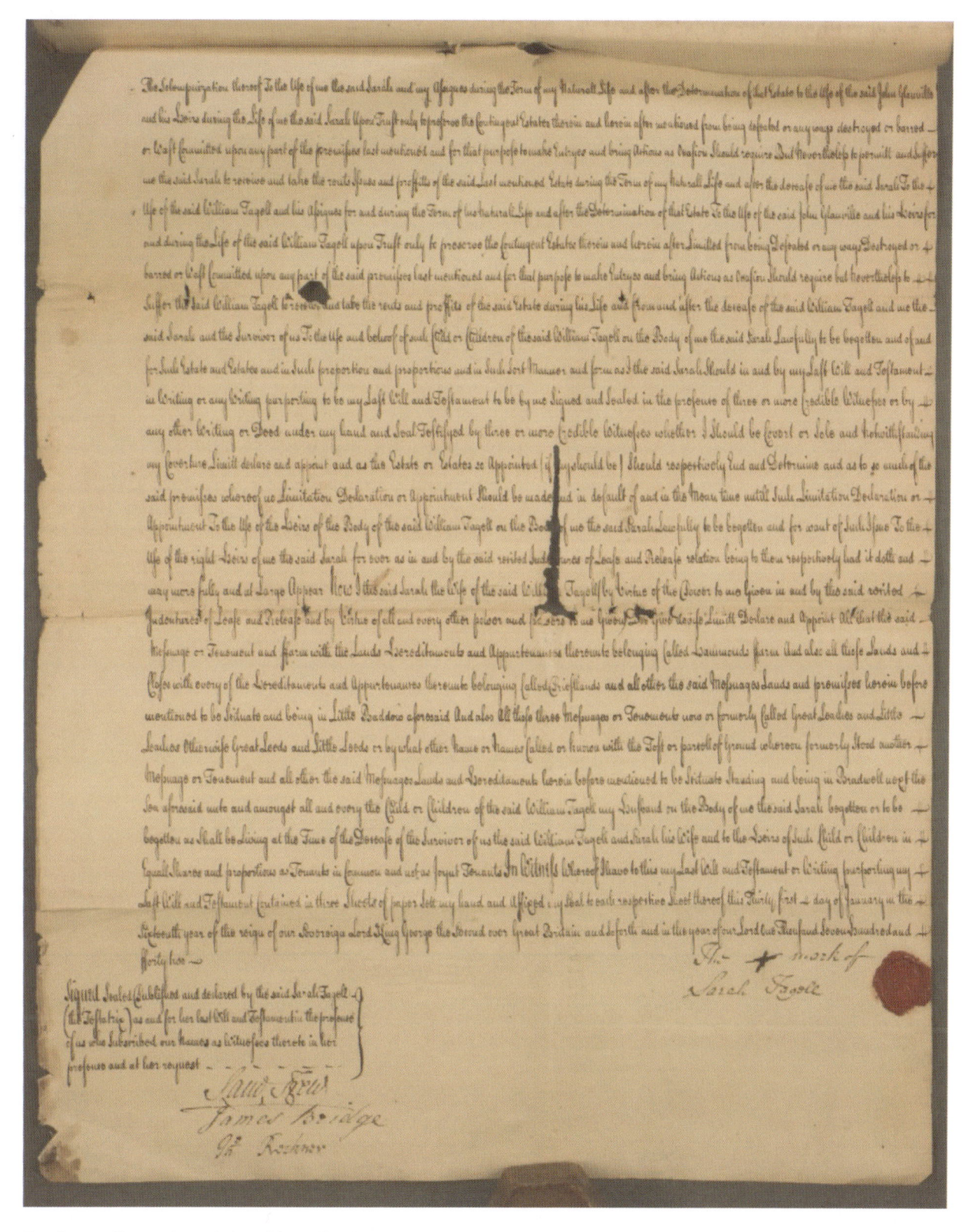

5. It confirms that John Glanville is an Edge toolman.

6. The will looks as if it was professionally prepared by a lawyer. Sarah is illiterate so we can not be certain to what extent she understands the document. There are long recitals concerning the terms of the Marriage Settlement. There are three witnesses and it seems to have been properly completed. We must assume the document is valid and William her husband has consented to her making it.

7. It only relates to her powers of appointment. It does not cover her ordinary free estate which I presume may pass to her husband William under an intestacy. Alternatively he may only

have a life interest. After she dies I doubt if it was proved in probate. The object is to get an appointment to her children.

8. It only covers the properties in Little Baddow and Bradwell on Sea. The Maldon property is not referred to but this is understandable. Sarah does have a life interest in that property if William dies but she does not at this stage have any power of appointment.

9. There is a clearer description of the croft in Bradwell on Sea. It is I think to the rear of 9 and 11 High Street. It adjoins the farm Delameers now Delameres which is to the south. It is to the west and south of the Kings Highway then called Bradwell Street now called Maldon Road. It is I think the land now forming the recreation ground and extending east to the Maldon Road. There was a tenant called Skingly in occupation of all properties. It looks like a standard 4 acre croft with cottage where the cottage has fallen into disrepair.

10. The will confirms that after her marriage Sarah Tagell has a life interest in the Bradwell on Sea properties and is entitled to all rent and profit until she dies.

11. The will refers to powers in the lease and release deeds entered into before the marriage settlement which I find a little odd. It does cover all other powers so this will include those in the marriage settlement. I believe that there are two daughters Sarah Junior and Hannah of Sarah Tagell alive and they are the only children of her and William. The appointment she makes is in favour of all of the children of her and William when they are both dead. These children take as tenants in common so if one dies then that share passes to their heirs.

5

1743 William Tagell case

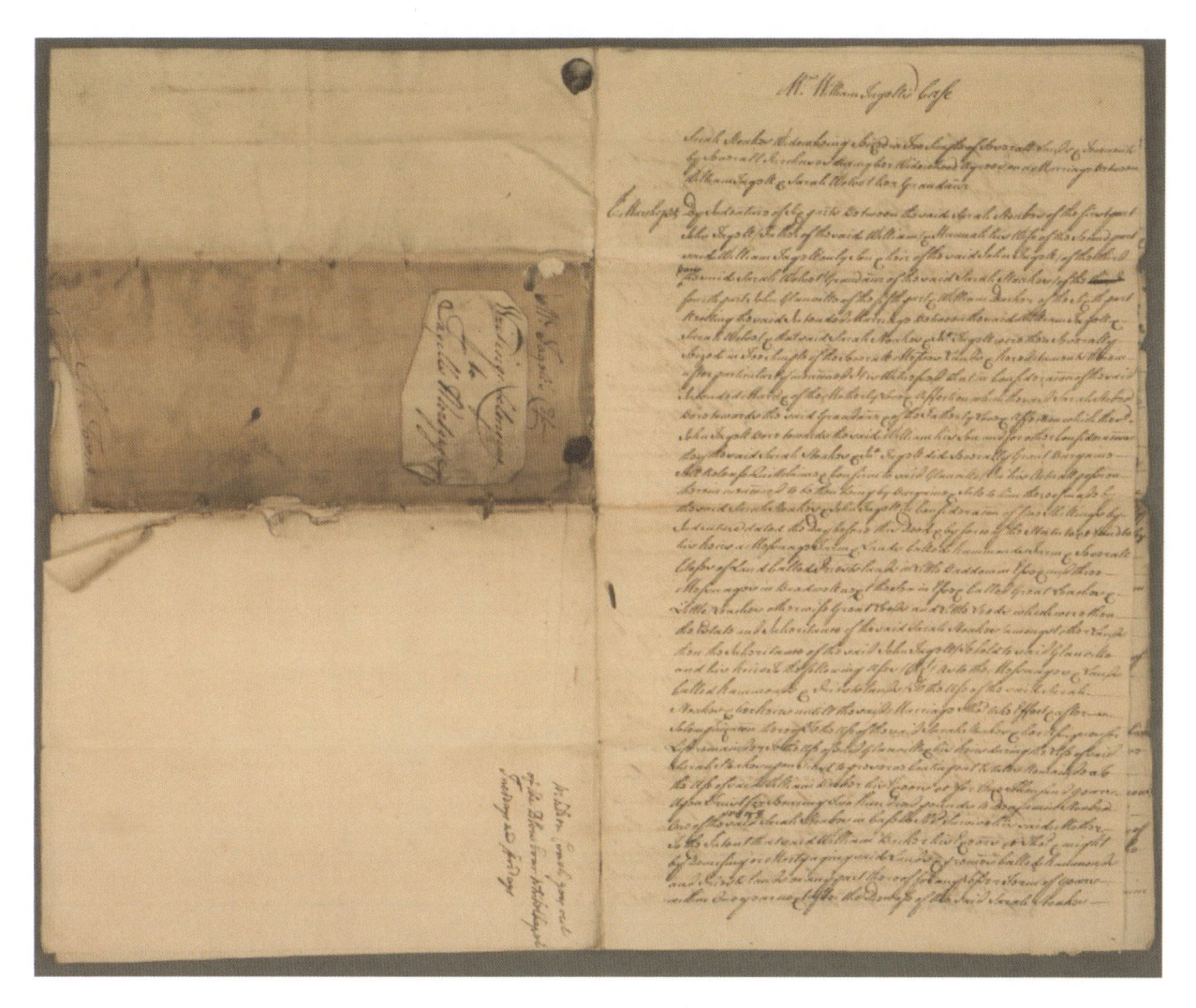

The document concerning this case is held by the ERO as a part of Accession Box A13186 and I make the following observations.

1. ERO had this document filed as 1743 William Ingell Case. They were wrong and hopefully they have now rectified matters.

2. The document is best described in modern terms. It is instructions to counsel with counsel's opinion.

3. The legal profession was similar then as it is today. They had solicitors/lawyers in towns like Maldon dealing with issues such as property transfers and wills. They in turn referred more complex matters to barristers who were more specialist. In those days they considered themselves to be socially as well as professionally superior to solicitors.

4. There is an endorsement on the back of the instructions that shows the papers were sent by coach from the Blue Boar in Maldon to Whitechapel. This indicates that the solicitor was in Maldon and the barrister in London. There was a coach going from Maldon to London on a Tuesday and Friday.

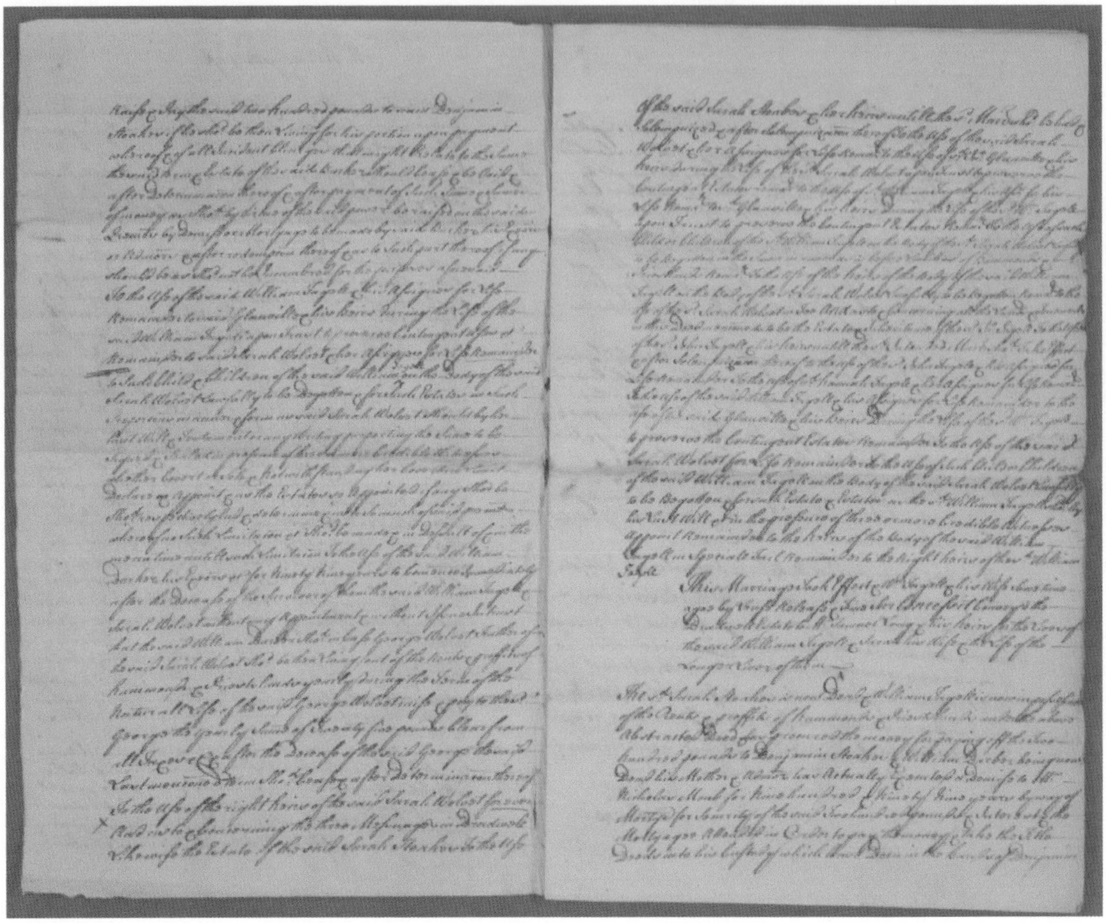

5. Sarah Stoakes as referred to in the 1735 Marriage Settlement the grandmother of Sarah Tagell made purchases of property during her widowhood. It is clear she inherited the properties in Bradwell on Sea so it could be that she bought the two farms in Little Baddow whilst she was a widow.

6. Between Sarah Tagell in January 1742 making her will and counsel giving his opinion in this case on the 10th January 1743 there was a conveyance of the Bradwell on Sea properties by William and Sarah Tagell to Samuel Long. This was limited to the joint lives of William and Sarah. They no doubt received a capital payment with Mr Skingly remaining as tenant.

7. William Tagell, Nicholas Monk his mortgagee and Samuel Long the buyer under the recent transaction of the Bradwell on Sea properties are worried about a claim being made by Benjamin Stoakes who was displeased with the terms of the 1735 Marriage Settlement. In common law he would not be the heir of Sarah Stoakes because she has an elder son and this was George Wolvett the father of Sarah Tagell

8. George Wolvett had gone to sea and had been missing for over seven years. I am sure the Tagell's wish to make a presumption he is dead. This will explain the limited contingency provision for him in the settlement. It also helps explain why Sarah Stoakes was bringing up her granddaughter Sarah Wolvett. George Wolvett may have been unhappy about Sarah Stoakes remarriage to Mr Stoakes.

9. The instructions to counsel imply that Benjamin Stoakes is responsible for the loss of the original lease. With this document missing there is a doubt as to the validity of the whole arrangement relating to the Marriage Settlement.

10. The opinion of the barrister is favourable to William Tagell and the other interested people. The loss of the lease is of no consequence. Its recital in the release is sufficient evidence of that it existed. The barrister bases his opinion on a case concerning Lord Grey that decided this very point.

1745 Assignment of mortgage and guarantee

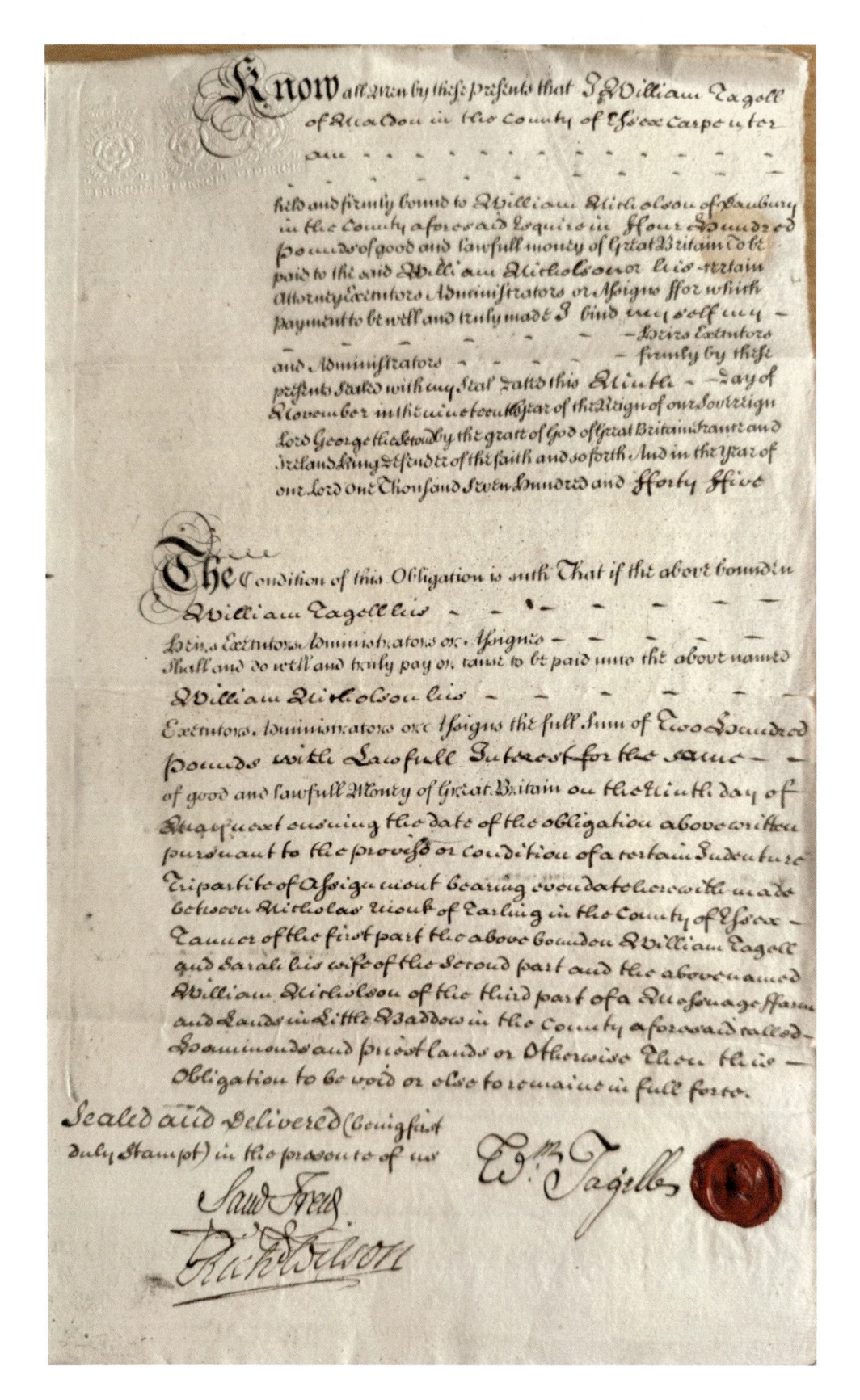

Know all men by these presents that I William Tagell of Maldon in the County of Essex Carpenter am .... held and firmly bound to William Nicholson of Danbury in the County aforesaid Esquire in Four hundred pounds of good and lawfull money of Great Britain to be paid to the said William Nicholson his certain Attorney Executors Administrators or Assigns ffor which payment to be well and truly made I bind myself my Heirs Executors and Administrators firmly by these presents sealed with my Seal dated this Ninth day of November in the nineteenth year of the Reign of our Sovereign Lord George the Second by the grace of God of Great Britain ffrance and Ireland King Defender of the faith and so forth And in the year of our Lord One Thousand Seven hundred and fforty ffive

The Condition of this Obligation is such That if the above bounden William Tagell his Heirs Executors Administrators or Assigns shall and do well and truly pay or cause to be paid unto the above named William Nicholson his Executors Administrators or Assigns the full Sum of Two hundred pounds with Lawfull Interest for the same of good and lawfull Money of Great Britain on the Ninth day of May next ensuing the date of the obligation above written pursuant to the proviso or condition of a certain Indenture Tripartite of Assignment bearing even date herewith made between Nicholas Mont of Parling in the County of Essex Tanner of the first part the above bounden William Tagell and Sarah his wife of the Second part and the above named William Nicholson of the third part of a Messuage ffarme and Lands in Little Baddow in the County aforesaid called Soammonds and priest Lands or Otherwise Then this Obligation to be void or else to remaine in full force.

Sealed and Delivered (being first duly Stampt) in the presence of us

Sam'l Frere
Rich'd Wilson

W'm Tagell

1. There are two deeds of the 9th November 1745. The assignment of the 1742 mortgage by Nicholas Monk to William Nicholson and a bond of guarantee by William Tagell as one of the borrowers in the 1742 mortgage. There is endorsed on the back of the assignment a deed of 11th June 1765 which I will deal with later in this report.

2. We have a new person involved William Nicholson. He gives his occupation as Esquire so he considers himself to be of some social standing. According to the historian Jill Goodson he died aged 54 on the 6th August 1750 and is buried at St John the Baptist Church, Danbury. According to parish records he had many children. Apparently the Nicholls family lived for many years in Danbury and in 1715 changed their name to Nicholson. This family had connections in Chelmsford and London. I understand at this time William Nicholson lived at Frettons in Danbury and his friend Edmund Fowler lived at Great Graces. Edmund Fowler features in the next deed to be considered.

3. The assignment in 1745 of the 1742 mortgage is a long document reciting at length the information we already have in the deeds. I doubt William Nicholson knows of the other information contained in the instructions to counsel in 1743. William Nicholson pays Nicholas Monk £200 and takes over the position as lender. A new date of 9th May 1746 is set for redemption (LN Mortgages). There is a particular reference to the right of re-entry on default which is significant. There could be a threat of foreclosure on the mortgage.

4. Lawful interest at this stage is still 5%. William and Sarah Tagell had not paid this but do so in full when the assignment is completed.

5. The guarantee bond by William Tagell is interesting in that it is a single printed sheet with blank spaces filled in. I have not seen this type of standard document being used before in such an old deed. It provides extra security and guarantees observance of covenants as well as the payment of interest. The guarantee is for £400 when the mortgage is only for £200 plus lawful interest. Before the assignment interest had been permitted to accumulate and this may be envisaged again. It was standard procedure for a guarantee bond to be twice the mortgage. The view in those days was there should be a penalty for default.

7

1746 Declaration of Secret Trust

1. This deed is in my view mistakenly dated. It says it is dated 16th January 1745 when it should be 16th January 1746. It recites the deed of assignment dated 9th November 1745. If it was dated 16th January 1745 this is impossible. You can not recite in one deed another deed that has not yet been completed. Why there was a delay between November and January in making this declaration of trust I do not know. Perhaps they are waiting for some default on the 1742 mortgage by William and Sarah Tagell. Only William Nicholson signs the deed not Edmund Fowler. I find this normal in these circumstances.

2. Edmund Fowler has the benefit of this declaration of trust. He was born in 1701 and died in 1751. He was the son of Christopher Fowler and Frances Mildmay. He original lived in Danbury but I think moved to Graces in Little Baddow in 1744 when he inherited that property from his aunt Elizabeth Waterson. Elizabeth Waterson is mentioned in the 1735 Marriage Settlement as the owner of surrounding land. The property Edmund Fowler inherits largely surrounds the two Tagell Farms in Little Baddow. He marries Elizabeth Patteshall on the 5th October 1744 and they have one child called Frances otherwise known as Fanny.

3. The declaration of trust makes our first reference to the two farms in Little Baddow being called Tagell's Farm.

4. The declaration of trust gives the occupation of Edmund Fowler as Esquire which would be appropriate as he owns Graces and is lord of that manor.

5. Edmund Fowler gives his address as South Sea House London. He is of course living at Graces so why he does this is not clear. Perhaps he thinks this adds to the mystery of his position.

6. The deed is straight forward. Edmund Fowler provided the £200 for the assignment of mortgage to William Nicholson and is entitled to this sum and the interest payable on it. I suspect he wants William Nicholson to keep his interest secret at this stage as he has a greater reason than just investing in a mortgage paying him 5% interest.

7. I suspect his real motive involves the fact that his land largely surrounds Tagell's Farm. He no doubt wishes to acquire Tagell's Farm and hopes to exert pressure as mortgagee to foreclose or threaten to foreclose if William and Sarah Tagell do not comply strictly with the terms of the mortgage and guarantee. I think they are already in breach by not paying interest on time. They will think the pressure comes from William Nicholson when the truth is the real lender is Edmund Fowler.

8

1760s History of Tagell, Sadd and Keys families

1. I chose 1760 as a convenient time to review generally some of the history of the family.

2. By 1760 Sarah Stoakes and John Tagell two of the original settlors in the 1735 Marriage Settlement (Settlement) have died.

3. Sarah Tagell the wife of William Tagell dies before her husband. We have already seen her will of 1742 which deals with her appointments under the Settlement to her children. Otherwise it appears she dies intestate. I presume her husband William inherited under the intestacy.

4. William Tagell also dies intestate. I find it strange that a comparatively wealthy man had not made a will.

5. William and Sarah Tagell have only two children Sarah and Hannnah. It is best we call them Sarah Junior and Hannah Junior. Sarah Junior was born in 1738. Her sister Hannah Junior was born in 1741. Sarah Junior dies in 1808.

6. There is a surviving Settlor Hannah the wife of John Tagell. I think she lived in the Parish of St Peters in Maldon. I assume that Sarah Junior and Hannah Junior go to live with her when their mother dies.

7. Sarah Junior marries John Sadd a carpenter from Maldon in 1760. He was born in 1734 and in 1765 they have a son John Tagell Sadd who dies in 1841. In 1763 Hannah Junior marries Gamaliel Keys a yeoman from Coggeshall then living in Wethersfield.

8. Sarah Junior and Hannah Junior inherit the estate of their father and their mother's interest under the Settlement. Since 1750 the inheritance rules stipulate with an estate like that of William Tagell his daughters as his only children should be treated equally. The interest of William Tagell under the Settlement has ended. He had a power of appointment in relation to the Maldon Properties that he has not used. There seems to be some tension between his daughters as will appear later.

9. The arrangement on the Bradwell on Sea properties with Samuel Long I think comes to an end because both Sarah and William Tagell have died. I think there are now conventional tenancies relating to all of the properties in the Settlement.

10. The business of John Sadd & Sons was founded in 1729 by the father of John Sadd born in 1734. The business became a Maldon institution. It started out as a small carpentry business and over the years it became a major timber merchants and builder. By 1780 our John Sadd had expanded the business into sawmilling and joinery.

11. On 7th May 1763 grandmother Hannah Tagell makes her will. The original is held by ERO reference D/ABW 102/2/7. She leaves all her personal estate to Sarah Junior. Sarah's husband John Sadd is the sole executor. Grandmother Hannah dies in 1766. This is the lady who allegedly signed the Settlement with a proper signature but now signs her will with a cross. This indicates she was illiterate or perhaps had some physical disability that prevented a proper signature. Grandmother Hannah makes no provision for Hannah Junior who presumably went to live with her husband Gamaliel up in Coggeshall. They may have moved to Bradwell on Sea by now. One assumes Sarah Junior inherits her grandmother's estate because she is living in Maldon and looking after her. There of course could be other reasons! It is only the personal estate that is bequeathed. Grandmother Tagell does not appear to own any property.

12. The ERO reference D/DRa L15/34 have papers and documents relating to the Court of Kings Bench action of the Crown against John Sadd Alderman. He has apparently

usurped and illegally exercised the office of Alderman from 8th January 1767 when he was elected following a meeting at the Moot Hall on 1st December 1766. He and his friend John Argent referred to later in this report with two other new aldermen were impeached. The position was made worse in 1768 when John Sadd was elected bailiff. The Crown then alleged because he was not a good alderman he could not be a good bailiff. The case is all about failing to comply with proper procedures about appointments.

13. John Sadd lives until the 6th April 1796 and is buried at All Saints and St Peters in Maldon. The son of him and Sarah Junior John Tagell Sadd marries a Sarah Harvey at Wickham Bishops on the 20th October 1795. John Tagell Sadd dies in 1841.

14. Hannah Junior and her husband Gamaliel have a son also called Gamaliel. He marries in 1794. His mother Hannah Junior died on 15th October 1795 and her husband Gamaliel then dies in March 1803.

15. I have not considered any of the law relating to the town of Maldon by virtue of its charter. This is not relevant to the deeds and documents being considered.

9

1762 and 1764 court orders and deed

1. We now have a series of court cases and deeds. Unfortunately I am not able to determine the precise purpose of these documents. There are possibly six court cases and several deeds. We only have two of these deeds that we can consider. Do not forget this where the lawyers made their money!

2. We need to go back and remind ourselves of the current position with the title. The 1735 marriage settlement made John Glanville the lead trustee supported by William Barker who died and was succeeded by his mother Hannah Barker. The settlement was for 1000 years. Nowadays this would be regarded as a virtual freehold. There has been no mention of the original trustees in recent transactions. The status of the freehold is uncertain. I presume John Glanville is dead and no longer has a watching brief. The mortgage of the 24th March 1742 was still subsisting. The benefit was with the Fowler family who I am sure wished to exploit their position.

3. In her will of 31st January 1742 Sarah Tagell (before her marriage she was Sarah Wolvett the person protected by the settlement) used her power of appointment in favour of her two daughters. Her daughter Sarah has married John Sadd (now Mr and Mrs Sadd) and her daughter Hannah has married Gamaliel Keys (now Mr and Mrs Keys). I assume the marriages were arranged and their husbands were men of substance The girls were in 1762 entitled to one half each of the property under the terms of the marriage settlement on a partnership basis being able to dispose of their shares separately. They also were coheirs of the estate of their late father William Tagell who died intestate. This is significant because he did not appear to have used his power of appointment over the Maldon properties presumably because his mother was still alive. The girls husbands became involved because as married women they only had limited rights so far as the ownership of properties were concerned.

4. We have Hannah Tagell the wife of the late John Tagell alive and in her 70s. Hannah Tagell was one of the original settlors in the 1735 marriage settlement. She has a life interest in the Maldon properties referred to in the settlement. She is entitled to the rents and other benefits from those properties.

5. In addition to Mr and Mrs Sadd we have John Argent involved with their half share and John Keys and Matthew Gosling involved in the half share of Mr and Mrs Keys. John Argent is a glazier from Maldon. We know he has close links with John Sadd because of their involvement in the local politics of Maldon. John Keys is a Yeoman from Weathersfield in Essex. At first I thought he might be the brother of Gamaliel who also likes to call himself a Yeoman. I do not now think this is the case because he signs his name and Gamaliel relies on a cross. It would be strange unless one has a disability to have two brothers one who signs his name and one that does not. My guess is that as they have the same surname John is a relative, perhaps a cousin. Matthew Gosling comes from Maldon and is a victualler. He probably has some connection with the Tagell family. Everybody is involved with collusive litigation. At one stage I thought that John Argent and John Keys might just fulfilling a role of White Knights assisting with the collusion. If so why has Matthew Gosling become involved?

6. The original of the deed of 29th January 1762 made between Mr and Mrs Sadd and John Argent held by the ERO in Accession Box A131186 has the same property description as the marriage settlement. After that the court papers refer to five houses, one croft, two barns, two stables, two gardens, two orchards, ninety acres of land and ten acres of meadow. It was common for the court papers to have vague general descriptions of the properties involved. The reference to five houses is misleading as only four are standing.

Presumably there is still a derelict house in Bradwell The tenancy arrangements indicate it is the Bradwell croft that may have been sold rather than the one at Maldon. Although there is a change in the acreage it is clear that it is the properties in the marriage settlement or the main part of them that is being dealt with. The property descriptions are on a catch all basis covering all potential interests of Mr and Mrs Sadd and Mr and Mrs Keys. They have no liability for waste. For example they could demolish a barn without anyone being able to object (LN Waste).

7. By 1762 the Little Baddow property known as Tagells Farm had a change in tenancy. William Hart has taken over that farm from Robert Martin. There are tenants William Sewell and Nathaniel Kether in Bradwell. If the croft had been sold I think they have a tenancy each of one of the two houses now known as 9 and 11 High Street. In Maldon the tenancies were divided so that the undertenants of William Tagell occupy the house with Thomas Knipe the croft and Isaac Davis the orchard.

8. As regards the three extracts of court cases we have one is in February 1762 and the other two are the same and relate to one of the cases in June 1764. The orders were in the Court of Common Pleas but the documents only contain parts of the information so we are not certain as to the exact terms of the judgements. They do confirm the agreements settling the cases were by way of Final Concord involving a fine. The Plaintiffs are friendly towards the Defendants. There is a term *Sur conusans de droit come ceo qie* used in these documents that acknowledges the Defendants have already given their one half share to the Plaintiff. They refer to a plea of covenant in the same court which indicates a separate action. It is all part of the same collusive litigation.

9. This was a time when there was some corruption in court cases. For example you could pay a court clerk speed money to get your case heard faster. Chief Judges were well paid at £2000 a year which equates to £500,000 today. Even so this did not prevent them and the court officials being bribed.

10. Rather than trying to explain in detail all of the law I refer you to the Legal Notes on uses, leases, quit claim, court of common pleas, fines and statutory powers. All these issues apply to these documents and are a lot of the standard terms you find in conveyancing in the 1700s.

11. The deed of 29th January 1762 by Mr and Mrs Sadd with John Argent is before the court orders but the deed of 2nd August 1764 by Mr and Mrs Keys with John Keys and Matthew Gosling is after the court order that year made in June. The order in June only relates to John Keys and it looks like further orders were required to cover both him and Matthew Gosling.

12. Although the two daughters of John and Sarah Tagell may have had differences that resulted in different cases being dealt with in 1762 and 1764 there seems to be concord that has given a similar result. Mr and Mrs Sadd and Mr and Mrs Keys have each been paid £120 which equates to about £30,000 today. This is the sum referred to in the court orders. I suspect other sums were paid. What John Argent and the partnership of John Keys and Matthew Gosling respectively receive in the way of ownership is not clear. Bearing in mind the consideration they have paid you would think they acquired some substantial interest. Nowadays bearing in mind that their interest only relates to a one half share it would be considered equitable in the nature of a trust. The trustees could then deal independently with that title from the freehold title. The deeds refer to wide powers such as a general power of appointment. These are similar to those found in the marriage settlement. There is a power to Mortgage the half share. There are covenants to cover further deeds that may be necessary. A barristers opinion may be required on this point.

13. This is still a male dominated society where husbands get a life interest first before their wives. Morally the property should belong to their wives as the children of Sarah Tagell. Mr and Mrs Sadd and Mr and Mrs Keys seem only to have a life interest. After the death of their parents the children of the sisters have a life interest. The provisions allow for the sisters to have children by a second marriage if their first husband dies. This honours the wishes of the original settlement. The default position is that the heirs of the sisters

take forever. This does tally with a variation in the 1764 deed allowing for the parents to creation of a lease for up to twenty one years at arms length.

14. To some extent this information reconciles with the facts that Mr and Mrs Keys mortgage their half share and in 1781 Mr and Mrs Sadd and Mr and Mrs Keys were able to sell the Freehold to William Hart of Hammonds Farm including the Priests Lands. The 1762 and 1764 deeds are referred to in various subsequent documents so they must have some significance. I can only assume this is all part of the collusive litigation that in reality brings the 1735 marriage settlement to an end and allows for a freehold sale in 1781.

Extract from the Court Order of John Argent, 29th January 1762

10

1765 Assignment of mortgage

1. We now have a deed dated the 11th June 1765 endorsed on the back of the second page of the assignment of Mortgage that is dated the 9th November 1745 made by Nicholas Monk to William Nicholson with William and Sarah Tagell joining in. Bearing in mind the status of the people involved I find it a little odd that this is being done by endorsement rather than a separate deed. This is I think explained by the fact that this deed of the 11th June 1765 was prepared at the last minute before Fanny Fowler married Sir Brook William Bridges the 3rd Baronet (Brook Bridges).

2. The mortgage of 25th March 1742 being assigned for a second time was in favour of Nicholas Monk who provided £200 (nowadays £60,000) to be paid to Benjamin Stoakes under the 1735 Marriage Settlement. In 1745 the benefit of the mortgage was assigned to William Nicholson who was secretly trustee for Edmund Fowler. I doubt whether William and Sarah Tagell and their daughters knew that Edmund Fowler was the true owner of the mortgage. After about twenty years I think this was still probably the situation. The two farms in Little Baddow I am certain are still a target for reincorporation into the Graces Manor Freehold Estate. The Fowler Family must have found it annoying having freehold farms next door to Great Graces owned by another family in particular one where the title had passed by female succession.

3. According to Wikipedia and the Jane Austen Society Brook Bridges and Fanny have a daughter Elizabeth 1773-1808 who marries Edward Austen Knight in 1791. He is the older brother of Jane Austen and she becomes a frequent visitor to their home at Goodneston. Edward has a different surname from Jane because he was adopted as a child by the Rev George Knight a rich relative of the Austen family. What is about to be revealed could have just come out of a Jane Austen novel. Like Mrs Bennett and her daughters in Pride and Prejudice I am sure the relatives and friends of Fanny Fowler were keen for her to marry a man 'the wealthier the better'. As Jane Austen would put it we now have a suitable match between two wealthy families. I think that we have facts that could be stranger than fiction.

4. We need to go back to 1735. The Marriage Settlement refers to the farms in Little Baddow being surrounded by the land of Elizabeth Waterson widow, the daughter of Colonel Henry Mildmay and his wife Mary. Elizabeth has a half sister Frances Mildmay so I presume that Mary died and Colonel Henry Mildmay remarried. He did have a son by his first marriage who died so Elizabeth becomes the senior member of the family and heir. Elizabeth married Edmund Waterson. When he died she had a dispute with his estate so there was no love lost with his family. Elizabeth made her will in 1742 and interestingly William Nicholson was one of the three witnesses. She died in 1746 aged 83. She had estates in Little Baddow, Danbury, Sandon and elsewhere. After a number of legacies and other provisions the bulk of her estate is left to Edmund Fowler her nephew the son of Christopher Fowler and her half sister Frances. Edmund Fowler like his father Christopher was a merchant and had numerous investments such as South Sea Annuities. You will remember that in the secret trust of 1746 he gave his address as South Sea House. He is becoming involved in this saga even before his aunt Elizabeth has died.

5. Edmund Fowler made his will in 1750 and died in 1751. After the payment of various legacies and other provisions the bulk of his estate goes to Fanny his daughter and only child. She takes at 21 or earlier marriage. His wife Elizabeth has a life interest in the residue of his estate. I think she dies between 1751 and 1765 because John Jolliffe Tufnell is appointed by the Court of Chancery to be Fanny's guardian.

6. The wills of Elizabeth Waterson and Edmund Fowler can be found in the *Sick in Body Perfect of Memory* book by John Bundock.

7. What is not revealed by the deeds is the fact that on the 19th April 1765 there was an Act of Parliament to facilitate the intended marriage of Fanny Fowler to Brook Bridges because she is a spinster and a minor. The Act covers her real and personal estate and conveys assigns and settles these estates in the manner specified. Amongst other things in Little Baddow it covers rents from the farms of Graces, Phillows, Aspfields and Cuckoos. The properties she owned I think were more than those in Graces Manor. I am sure that by this Act she loses much if not all of her power in relation to properties.

8. There are three parties to the 1765 assignment deed. The first party is Mary Nicholson. The second parties are Fanny Fowler and Brook Bridges her fiancé. The third parties are four trustees, John Joliffe Tuffnell and Sir William Mildmay, as nominees of the Fowler family and Lord Digby and Sir Thomas Hales as nominees of the Brook Bridges family. This deed concerns the £200 mortgage and is only a small part of the overall financial position. Before describing the purpose of the deed it is useful to understand the position and status of all the people involved. There are people and issues involving both wealth and power. There is reference in this deed to another indenture of the same date in six parts which I presume is a marriage settlement. Other than Mary Nicholson all parties to this deed are also parties to that settlement. Who the other parties to the settlement are difficult to determine due to damage to this deed. William DeGray the Solicitor General is involved presumably in a private not public capacity. There is also reference to another party being a Knight of the Garter. Information on the persons involved in the 1765 assignment is as follows.

The Nicholson Family

Jill Goodson says that William Nicholson died in Danbury on 6th August 1750. He was intestate and his son John dealt partly with the administration of his estate. He in turn died intestate and his mother Mary Nicholson the widow of William Nicholson living in Chelsea took over the administration of William's estate. This included the benefit of the 1742 mortgage held under the secret trust arrangement.

The Fowler Family

Edmund Fowler 1701 to 1751 originally lived in Danbury but moved to Great Graces in Little Baddow when he inherited the manor from his aunt Elizabeth Waterson. He married Elizabeth Patteshall on 5th October 1744 and they only had one child Frances. Edmund died on 25th July 1751 and his widow Elizabeth was the sole executrix of his will which was proved in the Prerogative Court at Canterbury. His widow Elizabeth then at some stage remarried a gentleman called Joseph Barbarous. She in turn died before 11th June 1765.

Frances Fowler referred to in the deeds as Fanny Fowler was born on 5th December 1746 and was five when her father Edmund Fowler died. She died on 16th March 1825 and was 78 a good age for that time especially after you have had a lot of children. The total varies in different documents from 8 to 13. Presumably she and her mother Elizabeth lived at Graces until at least when her mother remarried. At some stage John Jolliffe Tufnell was appointed her guardian by the Court of Chancery. In 1765 she was 18 and documents are signed in her maiden name before she marries Brook Bridges later on in the day of 11th June 1765. The deeds of 1765 say she is an infant because she is under 21 but she does sign documents on the same basis as an adult. A contradiction you would not have today. Fanny Fowler was also claims to be heiress to the title of Baron FitzWalter. This is an ancient title in the peerage of England created in1295. The viscountcy and earldom became extinct while the barony fell into abeyance. Fanny being female could never be Baron but could pass the title on to a male heir. This would have been attractive to Brook Bridges if he had in mind reviving the viscountcy and earldom.

Sir Brook William Bridges 3rd Baronet called in the deeds Sir Brook Bridges

He was born 17th September 1733 and died on 4th September 1791. He lived at Goodnestone Park near Canterbury, Kent. Modern photographs show it to be a very imposing house. He was a Member of Parliament between 1763 and 1774. He was 32 when he married Fanny Fowler on 11th June 1765. She was 18 but the age difference was normal in those circumstances and at that time. He was the half-brother of Elizabeth Digby and therefore it seems related by marriage to Lord Digby one of the trustees.

There are four trustees

John Joliffe Tuffnell

Lived from 1720 to 1794. He also was a Member of Parliament between1754 and 1761. He inherited Langleys Great Waltham Essex in 1758. He became one of the richest commoners in England renting out property in Essex and the North. We do not know when the Court of Chancery appointed him guardian of Fanny. He could have been appointed shortly after her mother died or alternatively this could have been some manoeuvre in preparation for her marriage .

Sir William Mildmay Baronet.

Was born in 1705 and died on 8th August 1771. He lived at Moulsham Hall with estates in Moulsham and Burnham-on-Sea. The old Barony had lapsed and a new one was created on 5th February 1765. There may be a family connection as Fanny's grandmother was a Mildmay before her marriage. He seems to have had an interesting life such as setting the limits of Novia Scotia in 1754 and making sure in 1756 there were two dragoons placed in the Church Tower at Burnham on Crouch every day watching out for the French fleet.

Right Honourable Henry Lord Digby

Lived from 1731 to 1793. At the time of these deeds he was an Irish Peer and because of this he was entitled to be a Member of Parliament. He lived at Sherbourne Castle another imposing property. In 1765 he became Baron Digby of Sherbourne. He was no longer a Member of Parliament but his peerage allowed him to sit in the House of Lords. Later in life he became an Earl. Between 1763 and 1765 he was Lord of the Admiralty. He would also be concerned as to what the French fleet was up to. He is I think related to Sir Brook Bridges by marriage.

Sir Thomas Pym Hales

Lived from 1726 to 1773. Another Member of Parliament. I am not sure how many trusts nowadays would have three Members of Parliament out of four being trustees. He lived at Howletts, Bekesbourne Kent. Not only a wonderful house but now more famous as the wildlife and safari park established by John Aspinall.

9. The mortgage assignment of 1765 is fairly straight forward. Mary Nicholson confirms she holds the benefit of the 1742 mortgage in trust for Fanny Fowler. For a nominal 10 shillings she assigns this to the four trustees. The part of the documents being examined has not been signed by William Mildmay, Lord Digby and Thomas Hales but as it is in three parts this would not be unusual. I presume this part is signed by John Jolliffe Tuffnell because he is Guardian of Fanny Fowler. The two witnesses of the signature of Mary Nicholson are different from the others. Presumably she had her own lawyers present. You can imagine a big meeting on the morning of the wedding with everyone present signing documents relating to the marriage settlement. Perhaps there were not many deeds to sign and this one was necessary as this mortgage assignment was not covered by the Act of Parliament. They may have discovered this at the last minute which explains why it is done by way of endorsement on the 1745 deed. There is a motive in that Brook Bridges has designs on acquiring the two farms in Little Baddow called Tagells Farm. The secret trust I think now becomes more public as no doubt the trustees would need to give notice that they control the benefit of the mortgage rather than the Nicholson family. A lot of paper work to cover what is now worth £60,000. Fanny Fowler would be worth millions of pounds today.

11

1766 Mortgage

1. The next deed is a mortgage dated 11th March 1766 and made between Gamaliel Keys of Bradwell near the Sea and Hannah his Wife as borrowers and William Hart of Little Baddow as lender. The loan is for £250 (this would be £54,500 today) plus interest. The statutory maximum of 5% still applies. The property mortgaged I believe is Tagells Farm Little Baddow. The deed clearly states Little Baddow but the name of the property is smudged. The 1760s is the start of the Hart Family having a strong non-conformist influence in Little Baddow.

2. The estate that Mr and Mrs Keys have mortgaged is their one half share in the property by virtue of the marriage settlement of 1735 and the court cases of 1764. Mortgaging a one half share that would today be regarded as an equitable interest would be unusual. There is no mention in this mortgage to John Keys and Mathew Gosling which supports the argument that they only have some reversionary interest. This deed of 1766 is in the nature of a conventional mortgage with a term of 500 years, a peppercorn rent and a date for redemption set on the 11th September 1766.

3. The first point of interest is that the lender William Hart is the tenant of Tagells Farm. I have never before seen a tenant lending money to a landlord who only has at best a one-half share in the property offered as security. It will be interesting to discover his reasons for making this loan. He may wish in some way to protect his position if he fears the motifs of the Trustees of Fanny Bridges as referred to in the Assignment of Mortgage dated 11th June 1765. This deed of 1766 acknowledges that the mortgage of 24th March 1742 for £200 has priority. It is confirmed that the benefit of that mortgage is held by Sir Brook Bridges by virtue of his marriage to Fanny the only child of Edmund Fowler. It is now definite that the trust between William Nicholson with Edmund Fowler created in 1746 is no longer secret. On the other hand he may have wanted to strengthen his own position as tenant or he may have just regarded the mortgage as a good investment. It was probably a combination of all reasons.

4. In 1764 Gamaliel Keys and Hannah his wife were living in Bradwell next to Coggeshall and he is still a yeoman. Now in 1766 they have moved to Bradwell on Sea and he is a victualler. Bradwell on Sea is where Hannah's great grandmother inherited property that is still part of the marriage settlement of 1735. There are the two semi-detached houses at 9 and 11 High Street and possibly a croft at the rear as part of the settlement. It looks like Gamaliel has disposed of his farm and acquired an inn. At that time there are only two inns of note in Bradwell on Sea. The Green Man down towards the sea and the Kings Head. I think he has acquired the Kings Head that adjoins the two semi-detached houses. This inn now has listed stables and a brew house immediately behind the houses. This could be where the derelict cottage belonging to the croft was situated.

Buildings and land in Bradwell on Sea probably where the Croft was behind 9 and 11 High Street.

12

1773 Plan explanation

1. This is a very detailed plan prepared at some expense. The original is held by ERO. From my experience this indicates that there was some dispute over boundaries presumably with Sir Brook Bridges the husband of Dame Fanny. There is an area to the north of the farms owned by Lord Barrington but all the other boundaries of the farms are surrounded by land owned by Sir Brook Bridges. From my point of view the significant issue is the plan acknowledges that the land we regarded as common land, now known as Waterhall Meadow is owned by Sir Brook Bridges. He therefore owns land adjoining Sandon Brook that then divides the original Hammonds Farm from the Priests Lands. It would have been inconvenient if you had to access the Priests Lands via Hurrells Lane. Sir Brook Bridges is still mortgagee of the farms. No doubt he is not keen on what he regards as commoners owning a substantial Freehold in his Manor of Graces. He also no doubt thinks that common land should be part of his estate.

2. The Plan is prepared by George Hutson Junior for John Sadd and Gamaliel Keys gents. It is a shame it does not acknowledge the status of their wives Sarah and Hannah. It states that William Hart is the tenant. The farm is no longer called Tagell's Farm and reverts to its original name as Hammonds Farm. The plan clearly shows what is now Hurrells Lane leading to Baddow end way which we now call Chapel Lane. Sandon Brook with its ford and the position of the properties of Waterhall and Diers alias Belmore Hope are identifiable. It also shows what is now Hammonds Road leading to Great Baddow. Hammonds farm house with its yards and orchard are also clearly marked. The roads comprise about three and one half acres of the area shown on the plan as the farm.

3. The table of contents shows a total area for the farm of just over 100 acres. The explanation refers to:-

   a. House and buildings coloured red.

   b. Yards and roads coloured yellow.

   c. Orchard filled with trees shaded green.

   d. Meads coloured green. This I think is just areas liable to flood. Nothing is said about any of this mead land being common land.

   e. Boundaries to the fields are shown in green.

   f. All water is coloured blue.

4. There has been some discrepancy in the papers considered so far as to the area of the farm. Ignoring the issue of common land and land comprising road and river the 96 acres in 1773 compares well with the 94 acres recorded in the 1735 marriage settlement.

5. I have considered the 1677 Map prepared for Sir Gobert Barrington and none of this farm comes within that map. The Chapman and Andre map of 1777 does cover this area.

6. There are clear maps of the Chelmer and Blackwater Navigation opened in 1797 but I cannot find any map showing the exact course of the river prior to its diversion to form the navigation.

13

1774 Deed of ratification and confirmation of mortgage

On the 7th October 1774 there was a deed of ratification and confirmation of a mortgage term for securing £350, (that would be £66,150 nowadays) plus interest and declaring new uses made by Gamaliel Keys and his wife Hannah (Gamaliel and Hannah) as borrowers with William Hart as the lender. It relates to their one half share in the whole of Hammonds Farm including the Priests Lands. I comment as follows:-

1. There is no mention in this deed of the 1742 mortgage now controlled by Sir Brook Bridges as the lender. This 1742 mortgage is referred to in the previous mortgage of 1766 and is still subsisting. Perhaps they decided it was best not to mention this as the 1742 mortgage relates to the whole of the farm. My view is that in any event the 1742 mortgage still has priority.

2. I find it odd that the Gamaliel and Hannah had gone to a lot of expense in 1773 in preparing a detailed plan of Hammonds Farm but the description of the property in this deed refers to the previous deeds of 1764 and 1766. Nowadays there are very few titles that do not refer to a plan of the property. William Hart must have known about the 1773 plan. George Hutson Junior could not have surveyed the farm without him knowing.

3. There is a contingency provision in this deed covering other land in Little Baddow and adjoining parishes as part of the mortgage so if there is a dispute with Sir Brooks Bridges this may be unresolved. Reference to adjoining parishes could be because the boundary line with Danbury was often uncertain.

4. Nowadays this deed would relate to an equitable estate. It does however mortgage all right title and interest in law and in equity to the one half share that Gamaliel and Hannah have in Hammonds Farm. I think it is more than just an equitable charge because it creates new uses.

5. There are full recitals of the 1764 deed involving Gamaliel and Hannah with John Keys and Matthew Gosling and the 1766 mortgage by William Hart as lender and Gamaliel and Hannah as borrowers. There is now reference to Gamaliel and Hannah paying consideration in 1764 to John Keys and Matthew Gosling. This supports the theory that Gamaliel and Hannah have a substantial interest in the property. There is a change relating to the uses as after Gamaliel and Hannah have died there is no reference to their children having an interest. This seems unusual as we know from subsequent papers they have a son. In 1764 the default provision was for the heirs of Hannah forever absolutely. It is now for the heirs of Gamaliel forever absolutely. This is contrary to the concept of female appointments contained in the 1735 Marriage Settlement.

6. Gamaliel is still an Innkeeper at Bradwell on Sea. The business maybe struggling as he has since 1766 borrowed another £100 secured by way of two bonds covering £50 each from William Hart in addition to the loan of £250. Details about these bonds are blank in this deed. I suspect they were for double the loan which was the standard practice at that time.

7. I notice that in 1766 Gamaliel marked the deed with a cross but he now signs the 1774 deed with his signature. In this period of 8 years he has learnt to write. This is the reverse of the position with Hannah Tagell who signs the 1735 marriage settlement (with what looks like the help of the hand of GOD) and then later makes a mark on her will.

8. In 1774 all the interest on the loans owing to William Hart has been paid and the rate is now confirmed at 4% slightly less than the statutory maximum of 5%.

9. I am not sure why William Hart should keep on lending to Gamaliel and Hannah. It could be a good investment. 4% is probably a better yield than the income from the farm. It could be that he likes having the influence of a mortgagee. I suspect it is a bit of both.

10. What we now have is a fairly straight forward mortgage arrangement. The original term of 500 years still applies but the 7th April 1775 is set as the new date for repayment. There are no special wording so once this date passes there is a presumption that the mortgage just still continues as a long term investment.

11. There is provision for further deeds to be entered into if required with a barrister to advise in that respect. Gamaliel and Hannah are not liable for past waste such as they or William Hart demolishing a building.

12. Samuel Lucas Bumpsted is one of the witnesses to the signing by Gamaliel and Hannah. We meet him again in 1781. I believe he is the solicitor based in Chelmsford for William Hart.

14

Who's who in William Hart's family

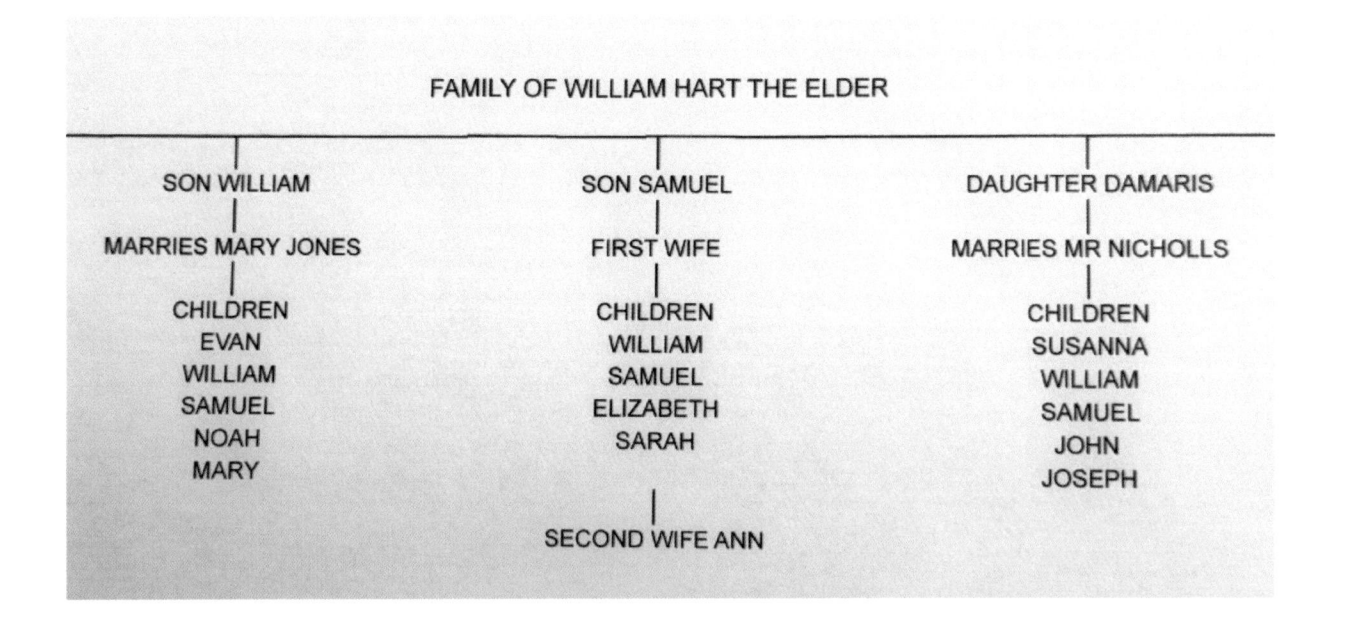

FAMILY OF WILLIAM HART THE ELDER

SON WILLIAM	SON SAMUEL	DAUGHTER DAMARIS
MARRIES MARY JONES	FIRST WIFE	MARRIES MR NICHOLLS
CHILDREN EVAN WILLIAM SAMUEL NOAH MARY	CHILDREN WILLIAM SAMUEL ELIZABETH SARAH	CHILDREN SUSANNA WILLIAM SAMUEL JOHN JOSEPH
	SECOND WIFE ANN	

15

1781 Four deeds

We have a major development in 1781 concerning the ownership of Hammonds Farm including the Priests Lands and the two outstanding mortgages relating to it. The first deed of the 7th August is the assignment by way of repayment and discharge of the mortgage where William Hart is the lender. The second deed of the 8th August is a lease by John and Sarah Sadd with Gamaliel and Hannah Keys (Sadds and Keys) to William Hart followed the next day by a release. The final deed of 9th August is the assignment by way of repayment and discharge of the original 1742 mortgage now owned by Sir Brook Bridges and his wife Dame Fanny (The Bridges).

I comment as follows:-

1. The result of the four deeds is William Hart has the right to the freehold of Hammonds Farm and the two outstanding mortgages are discharged.

2. There is a one year lease created on the 8th August followed the next day by a release. The Sadds and Keys as landlords sell the reversion of the lease to William Hart as tenant giving him the right to the freehold. This swallows up the lease but he only gets a right to the freehold that then needs to be confirmed by the Court of Common Pleas.

3. There are plenty of references in the documents to the *Sur Conusons* procedure which is basically contrived litigation where the defendants acknowledge they have already given their estate to the plaintiff. With this sale William Hart as plaintiff says to the court that the Sadds and Keys as defendants have agreed to sell the farm but are in default.

4. There are plenty of references to the deeds of 1762 and 1764 but John Argent, John Keys and Matthew Gosling are not involved with these transactions so their exact interest in the property is not known. One suspects there was even more contrived litigation at this stage.

5. Now if you think that is confusing the issue is made more complicated by the repayment and discharge of the mortgages. Both the mortgages were created by way of demise. One is a 500 year lease and the other lasts for 999 years. That is one year less than the 1000 years referred to in the 1735 Marriage Settlement. A straight forward discharge as you have today was not used. The mortgages have to be assigned for the remainder of the demised term. The lender needs to find a person to be a 'White Knight' trustee and then have the demise assigned to him for the remainder of the term. The guidance given on this procedure by the University of Nottingham is to look for the words in the assignment 'In trust to wait upon and attend the inheritance'. This is found in both the assignments so we can be satisfied that both mortgages have been discharged.

6. Now if you understand all of that you get a special award. The time it took to work this out is not helped by the 9th August deed of release comprising nine sheets of parchment and some of the most tortuous wording I have ever seen. Some previous documents have had very useful recitals. However I am now totally against those lawyers having been paid by the word!

7. William Hart a modern farmer in his day would have wanted to buy Hammonds Farm at the best possible price. In 1781 he has been the tenant of the farm for over fifteen years and should be regarded as a prudent buyer taking a long term view. In the twenty years since Sarah Sadd and Hannah Keys inherited the farm from their parents the agricultural industry has had difficult times. In the 1760s there were a series of bad harvests that led to rising food prices. The industrial revolution was still in its early days and there was

significant unemployment. This was not helped by conflicts abroad. The instability in America started in the 1760s that led to the American Revolution. There was a period of deflation and the value of the £ was reduced by 3% in 1780.

8. Gamaliel Keys had been an old fashioned yeoman farmer in Coggeshall before he moved to Bradwell on Sea to become an innkeeper. There is reference to him still farming in 1781. This may have been the original farm at Coggeshall or a new enterprise down at Bradwell on Sea. Whatever the situation he seems to have a frequent need for money raised by way of loans. John Sadd still has the carpentry business started by his father about 50 years ago. This seems to be expanding towards the major timber merchants it became. Finance for this expansion would no doubt be useful. It would be good to think that money from the sale of a farm in Little Baddow aids the growth of the Sadd's Empire. There were still major property investments in Maldon and Bradwell on Sea that formed part of the original 1735 Marriage Settlement. These would be of more interest to the Sadds and Keys than land in Little Baddow. I speculate they all want money for different reasons so a sale of Hammonds Farm is logical.

9. Now we need to summarise the payments being made in these transactions. A £ in 1781 is worth £215 today. Compare this with 1774 when £ was worth £189 today.

    a. William Hart pays a total of £1,550 which equates to £333,250 today. Deduct say £350 for buildings leaves £1,200 paid for the land which equates to £258,000 today. That price today would £2,745 per acre based on 94 acres. Ignoring the current hope value there is at the moment for Hammonds Farm I would pay for the land today £893,000. This is based on a valuation of £9,500 an acre. Agricultural land has proved to be a very good long term investment since 1781.

    b. Another comparison is the rental value of the land per annum. This has increased greatly. In 1781 is was 75p an acre but now it would be about £90 an acre.

    c. Of this price of £1,550 Mr and Mrs Sadd are owed £750 for their half share in the farm and Mr and Mrs Keys are owed £800 for their half share in the farm. Why they should be paid more you can only speculate. Hannah Keys no doubt still feels hard done by with her grandmother Hannah Tagell having left all her personal estate to her sister Sarah.

    d. Mr and Mrs Keys still owe William Hart £350 on their mortgage and need to contribute £135 to pay off The Bridges mortgage. They receive a net sum of £315.

    e. Mr and Mrs Sadd need to contribute £135 to pay off The Bridges mortgage. They receive a net sum of £615.

    f. The Bridges mortgage when it was created in 1742 was only for the sum of £200. It is now given a redemption figure of £270 to include capital and interest. Perhaps there has been an accumulation of interest. If there has been a dispute with The Bridges this may be part of a compromise. It is after all nearly 40 years since this mortgage was created.

10. The size of the farm continues to be an issue for me. These documents consistently say it is 94 acres and this includes an element of Common Land. This is of course consistent with the 1735 Marriage Settlement but not with the area of just over 100 acres shown on the 1773 plan. I accept all parties are may be in denial that the roads form part of the farm because of the liability to repair and maintain them. It is still a mystery to me that the 1773 plan and its measurements are not referred to. All the parties could want to forget its provisions if it was used to settle a dispute.

11. The first deed to consider is the assignment of the 7th August of the £350 mortgage owing to William Hart. It is made by him at the direction of Mr and Mrs Keys to Elias Pledger the elder a farmer in Little Baddow. Elias Pledger is the White Knight for this transaction. Mel Thompson has him farming 210 acres at Holybred Farm. Like William Hart he is a strong supporter of the Chapel and they seem to have a close bond. This deed makes no mention of the 1735 Marriage Settlement and the 1742 Mortgage. It does recite the 1764 deed as well as the mortgages of 1766 and 1774. Elias only pays

William a nominal 5 shillings for the assignment. William gives him a covenant relating to his title.

12. The second deed of the 8th August is a standard lease prior to its release the next day. It is made by Sadds and Keys as landlords and William Hart as tenant. It has the classic provisions for this type of deed. It is for one year at a peppercorn rent and a nominal 10 shillings in consideration is paid. This is nothing to do with William Hart's tenancy of the farm.

13. I will now try and limit what I say on the first deed of 9th August. This is the nine parchment sheets of release and conveyance made between Sadds and Keys, and William Hart. There is in it a very modern phrase in the deed referring to the sale being of a freehold in fee simple. This implies a freedom to dispose of the property as you choose. Rent has been paid by William up to the 29th September. It is not apportioned. His tenancy of the farm merges with his entitlement to the freehold today the 9th August. Any underleases he has created continue. Sadds and Keys give a 20 year commitment for further conveyance if need be. I remind you that a court order is still required to confirm this freehold transfer.

14. The final deed of the 9th August is the assignment of the £270 mortgage to The Bridges. This time it is William Hart's solicitor in Chelmsford Samuel Lucas Bumpsted who is the White Knight. He likes to call himself a gentleman as all good solicitors would do at that time. As previously mentioned they would have only worked Gentleman's Hours. He also pays a nominal 5 shillings. Technically this mortgage is still held by the trustees referred to in the 1765 assignment of mortgage. Three of these have died leaving John Jolliffe Tufnell the only surviving trustee. He was you will remember the Guardian of Dame Fanny before she got married. Now a days a second trustee would be appointed but in 1781 this apparently was not required. On the back of this deed there is an error referring to Sarah Sadd as Mary Sadd. I do like the idea in deeds that Dame Fanny the wife of Sir Brook Bridges is just called Dame Fanny. In the recitals there is no mention of the secret trust of 1746. The procedure followed is similar to the assignment of the 7th August that paid off the mortgage where William Hart is the lender.

15. It is some time since the farm was called Tagells Farm. We now say goodbye to the families of Sarah Stoakes, John and Hannah Tagell who made the original settlement in 1735.

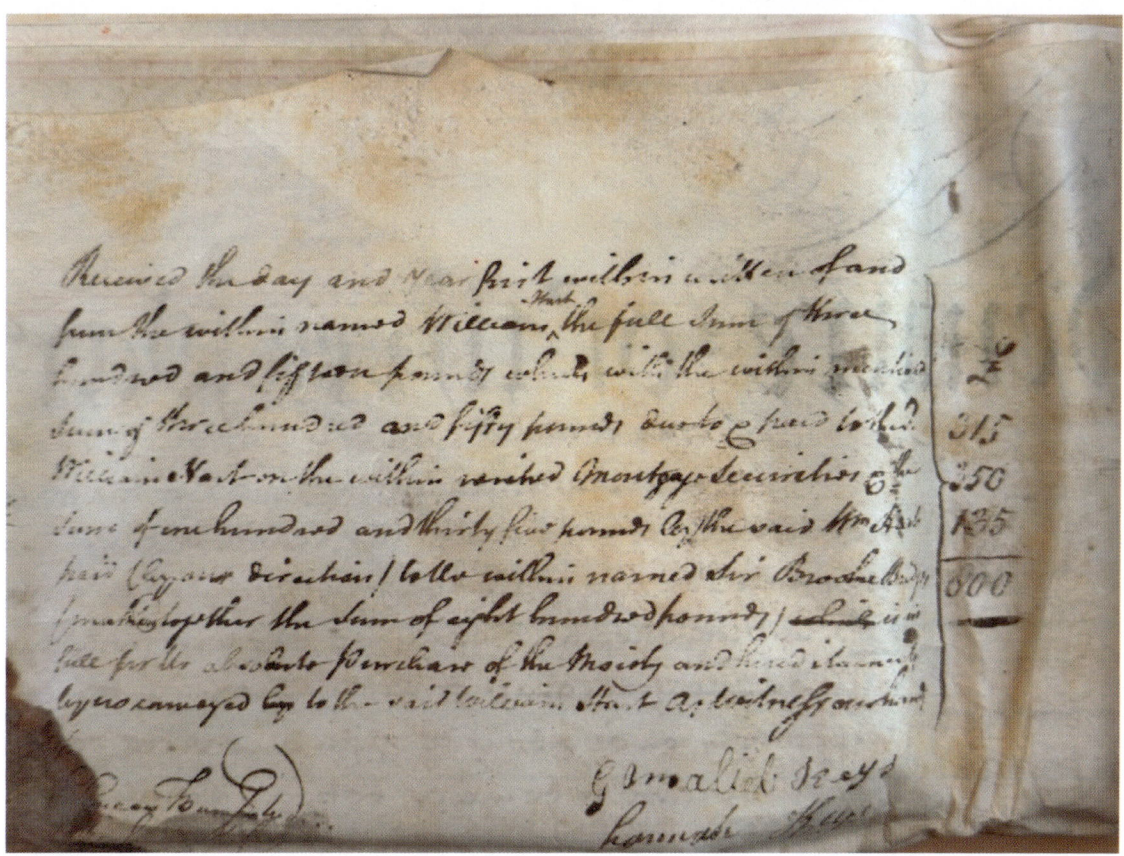

The receipts for Mr and Mrs Sadd and Mr and Mrs Keys for their half shares in the farm.

16

1795 Will of William Hart the Elder

We have an extract of his will proved in the court of the Bishop of London for parts of Essex and Herts that deals with the Priests Lands. This extract was obtained on 16th January1835 by a Mr Barlett on a payment of 5 shillings. This is proof that Samuel Hart had title to the Priests Lands by way of devise. The original will is held by ERO reference D/ABW113/1/71. It is dated 13th June 1795. Elder William died before the 13th November 1795 when the will was proved for what now would be probate. The extract is similar to an office copy of probate issued today and I consider would have been proof of title of Sammuel Hart to the Priests Lands.

It is now over thirty years since Elder William started farming both Hammonds Farm and the Priests Lands. First as tenant and then as owner. He likes to think of himself as a Gentleman rather than a Farmer. There have been some changes within his farming family. Elder William is still a staunch non-conformist. Evan Jones became the minister at Little Baddow Chapel in 1764 and his daughter Mary married the elder son of Elder William, William Hart Junior (Junior William). By 1795 Elder Willam's wife had died and also Junior William. Elder William's daughter Damaris Nicholls has also died. He is survived by his second son Samuel. We have no details of Samuel's children at this stage. Mary the wife of Junior William survives as do their children Evan, William, Samuel, Noah and Mary. Since her husband Junior William died about eight years ago she had been running the farm with Elder William. Damaris Nicholls is survived by her children Susanna, William, Samuel, John and Joseph.

I will give my interpretation of the will followed by comments that I make.

1. Elder William appoints two friends as his executors, James Stock of Hatfield Peverel and Samuel Boultwood of Woodham Ferrers. Whilst daughter in law Mary is in possession of Hammonds they act as trustees for that part of the estate. They then have special powers of management if she remarries or otherwise gives up possession whilst the trust for grandson Evan still is in place.

2. Provision is made for daughter in law Mary whilst she is in possession of Hammonds. I think this involves her farming as well as occupying the farmhouse. Her rights continue until 29th September after her son Evan becomes 30.

3. If she remarries, she loses her rights and the executors take over the running of the farm. I presume they can require her to vacate the farmhouse.

4. She occupies the 75 acres of Hammonds Farm rent free but she pays rent not exceeding £20pa for the Priest Lands. At Hammonds she and the executors are not to cut down trees except for elm needed for repair. She is liable for waste. (LN Waste).

5. Elder William desires that she pays the funeral and administration expenses.

6. Evan the eldest grandson of Elder William inherits Hammonds Farm on 29th September after his 30th birthday. There is a contingency for his heirs to take if need be and failing them by his brothers in age order. Until he comes of age the rent and profits of Hammonds are for the benefit of himself, his mother and his siblings.

7. Daughter in law Mary pays from the net rents and profits of Hammonds £20 for each child of Damaris when they reach 21. Then three years after Evan inherits he pays £100 to each of his siblings plus an annuity of £5 pa each for life starting two years after that. These payments are a charge on the Hammonds Estate. Evan also gets all of the residuary personal estate of his grandfather.

Extract of the will of William Hart, 1795

8. Samuel the second son of Elder William and his heirs in line if appropriate inherits the 24 acres of Priests Lands subject to the rights of his sister in law Mary to rent that farm while she still occupies Hammonds.

9. Samuel and his heirs and assigns if appropriate inherit the one third share that Elder William has in the sloop or vessel called 'The Prosperous'. This includes his share in the sails, masts, rigging and anchors etc.

10. There is £100 in the Bank of Merrish & Co in Chelmsford. Samuel receives £50. The other £50 is divided between the children of Junior William.

Comments on the will.

1. £100 in 1795 is worth £15,000 today.

2. There is little social improvement so far as inheritance is concerned. The first born still has priority. Evan as eldest son of Junior William the elder son of Elder William still gets the lions share of the estate.

3. I value the total farm at £2500. £500 (£75,000 today) for the Priests Lands and £2000 (£300,000 today) for Hammonds.

4. I assess the rent for the Priests Lands at 85p per acre which is £20.40 pa. The will says the rent is not to exceed £20 pa. It was at a commercial rate. I think Mary the daughter in law had a conventional tenancy.

5. £20 (£3,000 today) for each of the children of Damaris does not seem a lot. A £5 pa annuity for each of Evan's siblings is also a fairly modest provision from the income of Hammonds bearing in mind its value .

6. Evan getting the residue of the personal estate means he gets the furniture in the farmhouse as well as all the farm equipment etc.

    When the will is proved it says the personal estate is less than £300. This presumably is relevant so far as fees or tax is concerned.

7. It is unusual for Mary the daughter in law to be expected to pay the funeral and administration expense. You would expect these to be a burden on the estate. I think the executors are fellow farmers. It is not particularly fair for them to be expected to manage the farm without expense if they have to.

8. I am pleased to note the farm is now measured as 99 acres that is very near the 100 acres as shown the 1773 plan.

9. In 1795 a lot of boats were called sloops. Naval sloops had 3 masts. I assume this one is smaller perhaps 1 or 2 masts. It is difficult to see it as a boat for leisure purposes. A fishing boat I think is most likely. If it were a commercial boat the customers would not like it being called Prosperous.

10. When the will refers to rent and profits, there are sub tenants paying rent. I think there would be a separate set of farm accounts for Hammonds showing the profit that farm made.

11. There is an orchard that goes with the farmhouse but I do not see any other substantial areas of woodland. I am not sure what the concern Elder William had in this respect by specifying that trees were not to be cut down except elder for repair.

1798 Will of Samuel Hart

In the Name of God Amen! I Samuel Hart of White Notley in the County of Essex Farmer Do make this my last Will and Testament in manner following (that is to say) First I give and devise unto my Friend William Read of Beorchurch in the County of Essex Yeoman and to his Heirs and Assigns All those my Fields Closes or Parcels of Land commonly called or known by the Name of Priests Lands with the Hereditaments and Appurtenances to the same belonging situate lying and being in Little Baddow in the said County of Essex and now in the Occupation of my Sister in Law Mary Hart, her Undertenants or Assigns To hold the same unto and to the Use of the said William Read his Heirs and Assigns for ever Upon Trust that he the said William Read shall and do as soon as conveniently may be after my Decease sell and dispose of the said Lands Hereditaments and Premises with the Appurtenances for the best Price or Prices that can or may be reasonably had or gotten for the same and shall and do pay apply and dispose of the Money arising by Sale thereof and the Rents and Profits thereof until sold in such manner and to and for such Uses Intents and Purposes as I have hereinafter given and bequeathed the same Money And I do hereby will and direct that the Receipt and Receipts of the said William Read his Heirs or Assigns shall be a good and sufficient Discharge and Discharges to the Purchaser or Purchasers of the said Premises for so much of the Purchase Money as shall be comprized in such Receipt or Receipts and that after Payment of such Purchase Money to the said William Read his Heirs or Assigns such Purchaser or Purchasers shall not be answerable or accountable for any Loss Misapplication or Nonapplication of the said Purchase Money or any Part thereof but shall be absolutely discharged therefrom Also I give and bequeath unto the said William Read his Executors Administrators and Assigns the Monies arising by Sale of my said Lands Hereditaments and Premises and the Rents and Profits thereof until sold and also all the Rest and Residue of my personal Estate and Effects whatsoever and wheresoever desiring that all my Stock in Trade and other Parts of my personal Estate not consisting of ready Money may be sold and disposed of as soon after my Decease as conveniently may be Upon Trust that he the said William Read his Executors or Administrators shall and do in the first place by and out of the said Trust Monies and personal Estate and Effects fully pay and satisfy all my just Debts my funeral Expences and the Charges of proving and attending the Execution of this my Will and carrying the Trusts thereof into execution and after payment thereof Then upon Trust that he the said William Read his Executors or Administrators shall and do place out and invest the Rest Residue and Remainder of the said trust Monies and personal Estate in some or one of the public Stocks or Funds or upon Government or Real Securities in his or their Name or Names and shall and do pay assign transfer and dispose of the said Residue and Remainder of the said Trust Monies and personal Estate unto and amongst my Sons and Daughters William Hart Samuel Hart Elizabeth Hart and Sarah Hart equally Share and share alike as and when they shall attain their respective Ages of Twenty one Years And in the mean time my Will is that the Dividends Interest and Produce of their respective Shares of and in the said Residue and Remainder of the said trust Monies and personal Estate shall be applied by the said William Read his Executors or Administrators in and towards their respective Maintenance and Education And in case any or either of my said Sons and Daughters shall happen to die before they shall attain the Age of Twenty one Years

Witness.
Michael Fordham
John Scott
John Church

Saml Hart

without leaving any lawful Issue of his her or their Body or Bodies Then my Will is that the Part and Share of such of them so dying shall go to and be equally divided between the Survivors or wholly to the Survivor of them to be paid and the Dividends and Interest in the mean time applied in the manner herein before directed touching the original Shares of the said Trust Monies and personal Estate. And in case of the Death of all my said Sons and Daughters before such time of Payment without leaving lawful Issue of his, her or their Body or Bodies Then upon Trust to pay assign transfer and dispose of the said Trust Monies and personal Estate unto my beloved wife Ann Hart her Executors or Administrators for her and their own Use and benefit, And my Will and Mind is that the said William Read his Executors or Administrators shall not be charged or chargeable with or accountable for any more of the said trust Monies and premises, than he or they shall respectively actually receive nor with or for any Loss which shall happen of the same without his or their wilful default. And also that it shall and may be lawful to and for the said William Read his Heirs Executors and Administrators by and out of the aforesaid trust Monies and Premises to deduct and reimburse himself and themselves all such Costs Charges and Expences as he they or any of them shall sustain expend or be put unto for or by reason of the Trusts hereby in them reposed or the Management and Execution thereof or in relation thereto And I do hereby nominate constitute and appoint my said wife Ann and the said William Read Executors of this my will and I do appoint my said wife Guardian of all my said Children during their Minorities And Lastly I do hereby revoke all former Wills by me at any time heretofore made and do declare this to be my last Will and Testament In Witness whereof I have to this my last Will and Testament contained in two Sheets of paper set my Hand to the first Sheet thereof and to this last Sheet my Hand and Seal the Twenty sixth Day of September in the Year of our Lord One Thousand seven Hundred and Ninety eight

Signed Sealed Published and Declared by the said Samuel Hart the Testator as and for his last Will and Testament in the Presence of us, who at his request in his Presence and in the Presence of each other have hereunto subscribed our Names as Witnesses thereto

Samuel Hart

Michael Sordham
John Scott
John Church

This is the original of the will of Samuel Hart the second son of William Hart the elder of Hammonds. The will is dated the 29th of September 1798. He is a farmer in White Notley, Essex. There is no evidence of registration with one of the church courts or of revocation of this will. Samuel Hart died sometime before the 19th December 1804 as the ERO have evidence that his special trustee and executor William Reed entered into deeds on that day in relation to the Priests Lands. William Reed may not have needed to register the will to deal with that transaction because he had title by way of a devise to him in the will. Samuel has another executor his wife Ann who is also appointed guardian of his children whilst they are minors. He has four children William Hart, Samuel Hart, Elizabeth Hart and Sarah Hart.

His friend William Reed is a yeoman living in Beerchurch (I presume this is Berechurch near Colchester) Essex. He has the responsibility of selling the Priest Lands subject to the tenancy in favour of Samuel's sister in law Mary Hart when convenient for the best possible price. Mary Hart may have undertenants. He is then responsible for investing the proceeds of sale along with the proceeds of Samuel's personal estate in public stocks or funds. Alternatively investment could be in government or real securities. The proceeds of sale of Priests Lands includes rent and profits. The personal estate to be sold includes the stock in trade of Samuel. His children take their share when they reach 21 years. Income may be used for their maintenance and education. If one child dies leaving issue they take that share. Failing that the surviving siblings share but if none the residue passes to his wife Ann.

William Reed is entitled to deduct from the residue the costs of administration and is not liable for any loss unless he wilfully defaults.

No mention is made of Samuel's one third share in the vessel Prosperous. Perhaps this has already been sold. I think that Samuel was a tenant farmer at White Notley as there is no mention of the disposal of that property in his will.

There is no direct provision for Ann his wife in this will which I find odd. Perhaps she has independent means. As she is guardian for the children I assume she is not their mother. Presumably there was a first wife who has died and Ann is the second wife.

1804 Assignment of lease

This Indenture of Three parts made the Twelfth Day of November in the Year of our Lord One Thousand Eight hundred and four Between Mary Hart of Little Waddow in the County of Essex Widow of the first part William Hart of the same place Sawyer Samuel Hart of the Hamlet of Moulsham in the Parish of Chelmsford in the said County Carpenter Evan Hart of Little Waddow aforesaid farmer Noah Hart of Bedford Street Norwich Rood Soho in the County of Middlesex Bachi maker Richard Choat of Chelmsford yeoman and carpenter and Mary his wife (which said William Hart Samuel Hart Evan Hart Noah Hart and Mary Choat are the Sons and Daughter of the said Mary Hart) of the second part and Jeremiah Pledger of Little Waddow aforesaid Gentleman of the Third Part Whereas the said Mary Hart is under and by virtue of the Last Will and Testament of William Hart late of Little Waddow aforesaid farmer deceased the father of William Hart late of the same place farmer her late Husband deceased entitled to the unexpired Term of Four Years from Michaelmas last past of and in a certain Farm called Hammonds situate near Graces Wall in the Parish of Little Waddow aforesaid and also to certain Lands called Quest Lands situate near the said farm and now in her own Occupation And whereas the said Mary Hart together with the said William Hart Samuel Hart Evan Hart Noah Hart Richard Choat and Mary his wife who are interested in the produce proceeds and profits arising from the said Farm and Lands for the said Term of Four Years from Michaelmas last have mutually agreed between themselves immediately to sell and dispose of the said Term of Four Years of and in the said Premises together with the Turnips Young Clovers Tares and Rye now growing on the said Premises as also the Dung and Fallows in and about the said Premises And whereas the said Jeremiah Pledger hath contracted and agreed to and with the said Mary Hart by and with the Consent approbation and goodwill of the said William Hart Samuel Hart Evan Hart Noah Hart and Richard Choat and Mary his wife testified by their being severally parties to and sealing and delivering these presents for the unexpired Term of Four Years from last Michaelmas of and in the aforesaid Farm now erected Cottage and premises and for all and every the Turnips Young Clovers Tares and Rye now sown and growing in or and about the said Premises and the said Dung and Fallows thereon at or for the price or sum of Five Hundred and Twenty five pounds Now this Indenture witnesseth that in pursuance of the said agreement and for and in consideration of the sum of Five Hundred and Twenty five pounds of lawful Money of the Currency of Great Britain to her the said Mary Hart in hand well and truly paid by the said Jeremiah Pledger at the request and by the direction and appointment of the said William Hart Samuel Hart Evan Hart Noah Hart and Richard Choat and Mary his wife (testified as aforesaid) at or before the sealing and delivery of these presents the receipt and payment whereof she the said Mary Hart as also the said William Hart Samuel Hart Evan Hart Noah Hart and Richard Choat and Mary his wife testified as aforesaid Do and each and every of them doth hereby unequivocally admit acknowledge acquit release exonerate and forever discharge the said Jeremiah Pledger his Heirs Executors Administrators and assigns and each

The next deed is dated the 12th November 1804 and is made by Mary Hart and her children assigning a lease made on 29th September 1804 to Jeremiah Pledger. The deed was prepared by Copland lawyers of Chelmsford. It is in very small print and parts are illegible. I comment as follows.

1. We firstly need to go back to the will of William Hart the Elder of 1795. Evan his eldest grandson inherits the Freehold of Hammond's Farm on the 29th September after his 30th birthday. My guess is that this will be the 29th September 1808 when the assigned lease expires. Having said that it appears that Evan wishes to leave Hammonds Farm the sooner the better. Perhaps his marriage in 1804 to Phyliss Lince of Great Baddow had an impact on his position. He is no longer the first named child in the assignment. His mother Mary Hart is probably not very pleased with him. She has spent a lot of time keeping the farm going and preserving his inheritance. She is naturally disappointed that he does not wish to continue to run the farm.

2. Mary Hart is the daughter in law of William Hart the Elder her husband William Hart Junior having died. Under the will she occupies Hammonds Farm rent free and pays rent not exceeding £20 pa on the Priests Lands.

3. The siblings of Evan Hart have various interests under the will of William Hart the Elder including a payment of £100 each three years after Evan inherits with a further annuity of £5 pa each for life starting two years after that.

4. Samuel Hart the second son of William Hart the Elder has inherited the Freehold of the Priests Lands

5. On the 29th September 1804 a lease was created in favour of Mary Hart, rent free for Hammonds and at a rent of £20 pa for the Priests Lands for four years. We do not have a copy of this lease but all relevant members of the Hart Family or their executors were no doubt involved. It is this lease that Mary Hart assigns to Jeremiah Pledger who likes to call himself a gentleman and is living in Little Baddow.

6. Mary Hart still has 4 sons and a daughter Mary. The daughter has married and enters this assignment in conjunction with her husband Richard Choat. Her son William is a Sawyer living at Hammonds. Her son Samuel is a Carpenter living in Moulsham Chelmsford. Her son Evan the heir to Hammonds is farming and living there. Lastly her son Noah is a Coachmaker and has moved to Soho which at that time was in Middlesex. The children enter into the assignment to ratify and approve the action of their mother. They receive a nominal payment of 10 shillings each under the terms of the deed and other consideration which is not specified. Perhaps some of the money paid to their mother is distributed amongst them.

7. The description of Hammonds Farm says that it is near Grace's Walk and the Priest Lands are near Hammonds Farm which includes a newly erected cottage. May be this cottage at Hammonds is somewhere for Mary to live when Jeremiah moves into the farmhouse.

8. One of the interesting things about this assignment is the description of the farming activities. Included in the sale are the Turnips, Young Clover, Tares and Rye sown and growing. Tares are an annual fast growing vetch legume a member of the pea family. These are all good cash crops to sell to people like dairy farmers for feeding their cattle in winter.

9. The farms were operating on a then modern crop rotation. Jeremiah had to farm in a husband like manner in accordance with the custom of the county. He is liable for any taxes. The assignment acknowledges that some fields are fallow and Jeremiah needs to leave not more than 10/12 acres fallow properly ploughed and farrowed when his lease ends.

10. Jeremiah pays Mary £525. The pound today was worth £125 in 1804. The consideration today would be £65,625.00. This is free of any debts or liabilities and Jeremiah will have the benefit of any rents from undertenants. This appears to be a reasonable payment bearing in mind the payments made to Mary's children. For example four years rent on the fields at Hammonds at £1 pa an acre comes to £300 which would be £37,500 today. This leaves a balance of £225 to cover all the buildings including the new cottage. Jeremiah is also paying rent of £20pa to Samuel Hart for the Priests Lands. There is no farmhouse with that farm. I suspect part of the payment is to keep the Hart family sweet towards him. This assignment

does of course give Jeremiah a foot in the Hammonds door. From subsequent history we know of his ambitions.

11. In 1803 there has been a general survey of assets because the County feared that there would there would be an invasion by Napoleon. Mary Hart was using a substantial part of the farms for keeping animals as well as growing arable crops. She had 6 cows, 3 young cattle and colts, 52 sheep and goats and 17 pigs. She also had 4 draft horses, 2 wagons and 3 carts. I presume these assets may have been included in the assignment to Jeremiah Pledger but as they are not referred to in the deed they could have been disposed of separately.

This section of the document shows the diversity of crops on the farm, including turnips, clover, tares and rye. This was unusual for an Essex farm at the beginning of the 19th century, when the growing of corn predominated.

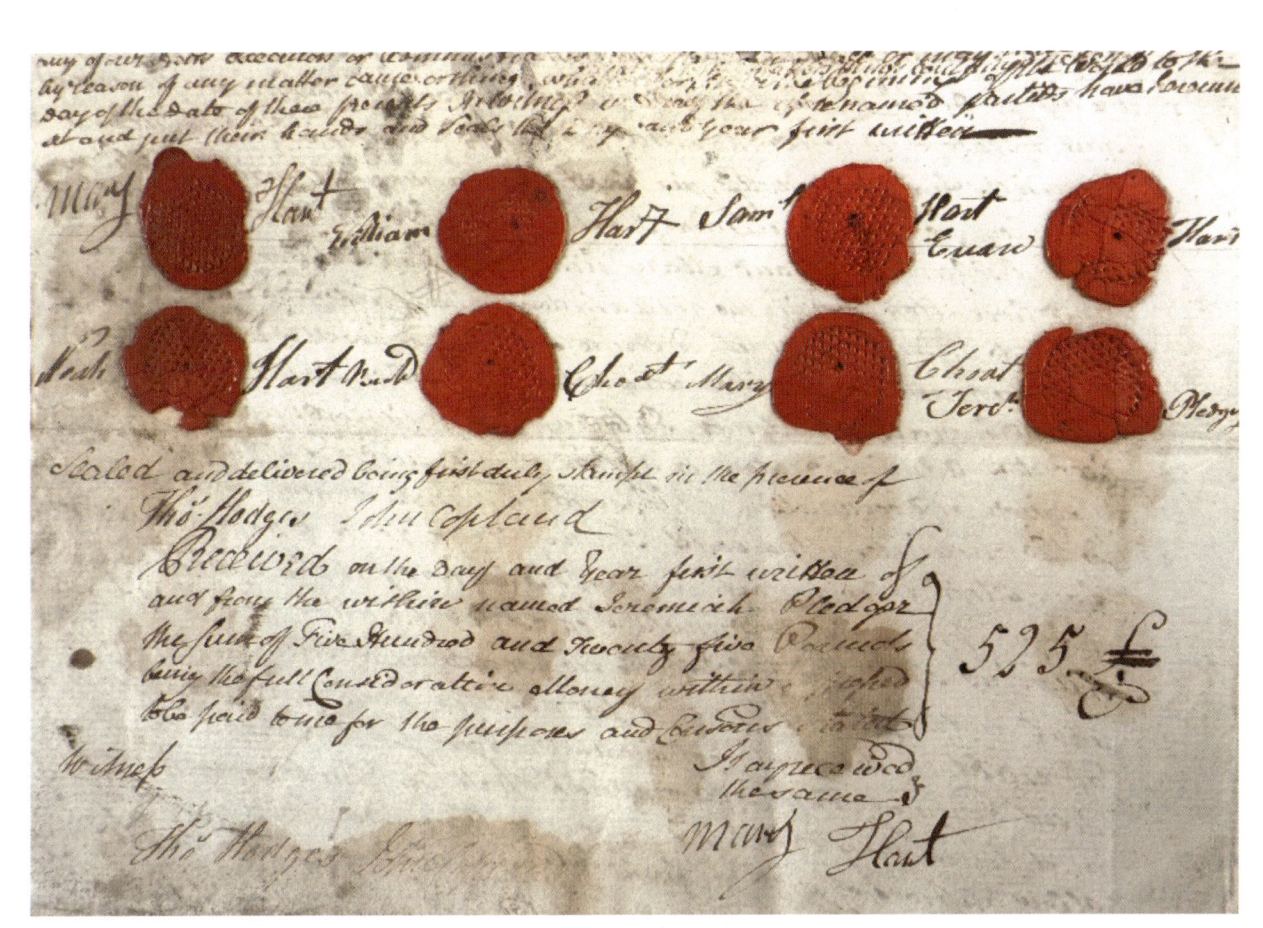

This is the receipt of Mary Hart for the payment of £525.00.

19

1804 Lease and Release

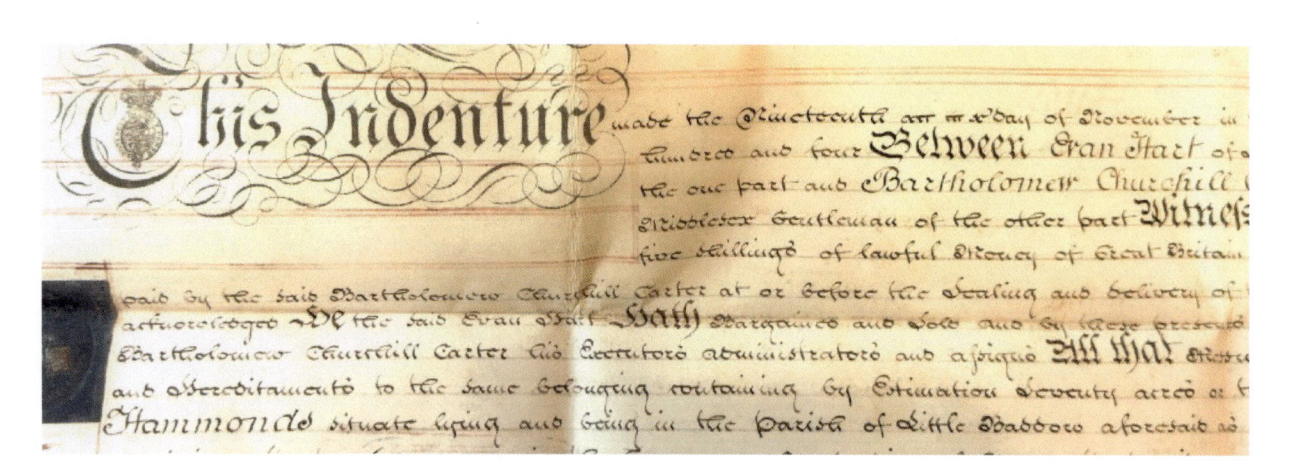

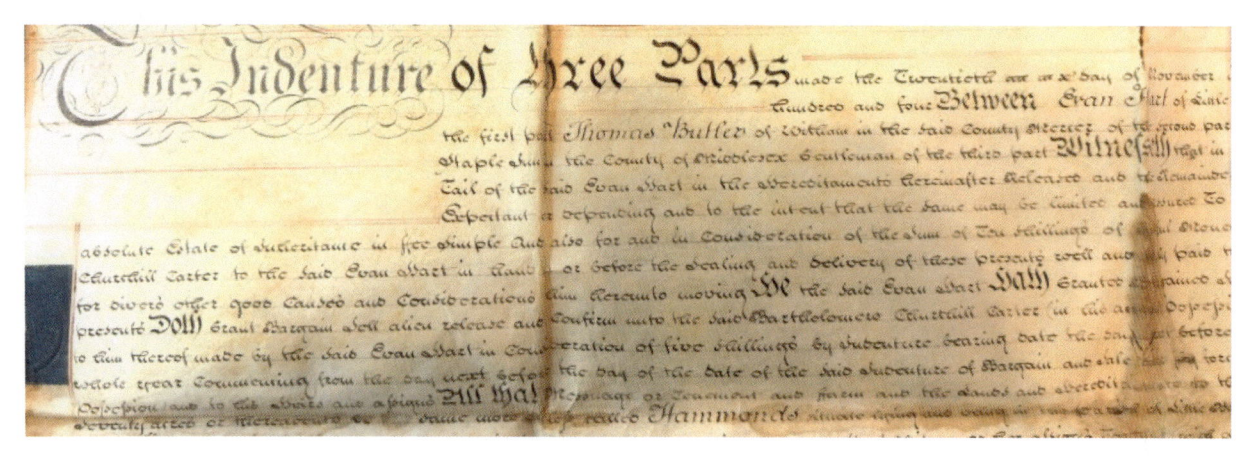

Extracts of the lease and release documents showing their dates.

We now have two deeds a lease dated the 19th November 1804 and a release dated the 20th November 1804. This is a procedure to release Evan Hart from the condition in the will of his grandfather William Hart the Elder that prevents him from inheriting the Freehold of Hammonds Farm until he is past 30 years old. I will confine myself to a description of the deeds because it would be very complex to describe the court actions that go with them. I suspect that we are only looking at two out of three deeds. There was I think a third deed after the court actions that would have confirmed the true owner of Hammonds Farm.

PEOPLE INVOLVED

1. Evan Hart is still living in Little Baddow and is described as a farmer. I am not sure where he is living and farming because at this stage Jeremiah Pledger is the occupier of Hammonds Farm by virtue of the assignment to him of the 4 year lease created for Mary Hart the daughter in law of William Hart the Elder. Perhaps he, his new wife and mother are living in the new cottage at Hammonds Farm and he is helping out on this farm and/ or the Priest Lands. I still think Evan is not 30 until 1808 that is 13 years after his

grandfather died. That makes Evan about 17 when his grandfather made his will. I presume that there was something about the personality or character of Evan that caused his grandfather to make the conditions as specified in his will of the 13th June 1795. Nowadays you might have inheritance restricted until after a man reaches 25 but 30 I consider would be unreasonable.

2. Bartholomew Churchill Carter of Staple Inn Middlesex likes to call himself a Gentleman but I am sure he is a lawyer. As previously mentioned in this report he will no doubt have only worked 'Gentleman's Hours'. With this type of transaction it was common for the lawyer handling the case to be what is called 'the Tenant to the Praecipe'. The last deed we looked at dated 12th November 1804 was prepared by Copland a popular lawyer in Chelmsford with non conformists. This type of procedure of barring an entail would normally be something that was pursued by the upper classes. The action now required would need a specialist lawyer like Bartholomew Carter based In London.

3. Thomas Butler of Witham is the third party involved. He may be a buyer of the Freehold or just a White Knight acting as a nominee/trustee as I will discuss later. I think he describes himself as a Mercer. I suppose with the establishment of Courtaulds near Braintree in 1799 we have a number of traders in fine cloth in the area. Janet Gyford in her history of Witham Fires of 1820 refers to a wealthy dissenter working as a grocer, draper and farmer called Thomas Butler. I think this must be the same person. There is a history of people in this report giving the best description of their occupation. So a draper being a mercer is no different.

THE PROPERTY

It is only Hammonds Farm involved with this transaction not the Priests Lands. This procedure only requires a vague description of the property so it is not surprising we go back to a reference to an acreage of 70 rather than 75 which I believe is the correct figure. There is a more detailed description of what is included in the Hammonds Estate including it rents and profits. Mary Hart and her assigns are referred to as being in occupation. Jeremiah Pledger her assignee is now in occupancy. As this whole procedure is collusive I presume that Bartholomew Carter and Thomas Butler are aware of the position. Disclosing this to the court would I consider just complicate the issue. It is probably best the court does not know the true position.

THE PURPOSE

The main purpose of these deeds is to bar and destroy the age limitation of the inheritance of Evan Hart having to wait until he is 30 years old so the freehold is vested in him without conditions now. This is similar to barring an entail. This is achieved by the following process. I promise I am trying to make this simple!

1. Like the procedure for Final Concord we have already considered this is another form of collusive litigation.

2. For all intents and purposes the two deeds considered are one transaction.

3. The lease of 19th November is much as we would expect. Despite referring to two years on the back sheet it is for one year at a peppercorn rent. The bargain and sale refers to the nominal consideration of 5 shillings.

4. The release of the 20th November again has a nominal consideration of 10 shillings but refers to other good cause and consideration.

5. The actions in court start in Chancery and are then transferred to the Court of Common Pleas. One of the writs required referred to in the release deed has the interesting title *Sur Diseisim en le Post* acknowledging the right of recovery.

6. Bartholomew Carter is the tenant to the praecipe. The judge orders that Thomas Butler has the right of recovery against him. Thomas Butler then has the right to release the reversion to Evan Hart. I am refraining from explaining the complexity of the court cases that achieve this outcome.

7. The release deed ends with the declaration that Evan Hart owns the freehold.

8. The question is then is there another deed confirming the position of Thomas Butler as buyer or was he in complete cahoots with Evan Hart just acting as nominee/trustee to break the limitation resulting in the inheritance by Evan Hart of the freehold without condition? Well little in these documents was ever straightforward so it is probably fitting it ends with an unanswered question.

20

LEGAL NOTES

I will deal with aspects of the law that I consider are relevant to these deeds and documents. There was not much change in land law in the 1700s. These notes are just to give you some background to the law. They are a brief summary.

HISTORY OF THE LAW

1. I have made reference to the farms in Anglo Saxon times. They may date from early times. I have not considered Roman or Anglo Saxon law. I have not considered the law relating to towns and churches as I do not think this is relevant.

2. The Norman Conquest is I think the best place to start. William the Conqueror owned all the land and under the feudal system the monarch granted estates to the Lords who then created a chain of tenancies starting with Lords of the Manor. In 1066 most people were slaves who then became serfs. Only 12% of the population were considered Freemen. Freemen existed prior to the conquest. After Magna Carta common land rights were acknowledged. The Black Death changed much with surviving peasants having greater power.

3. From these medieval times the manorial system evolved. Land transactions could be enrolled locally via manorial courts or in the central courts. This included sales, leases, mortgages, settlements and the inheritance of land. Property rights involving third parties became important.

4. I think that Hammonds Farm and the Priests Lands were Freehold from Norman Times. There is reference to Hammonds Farm definitely being Freehold in the 1500s. Land was still power in Tudor England but after that its economic and political importance diminished.

5. From these Freehold estates evolved customary leaseholds such as copyhold and conventional leaseholds.

    A. With copyhold rent was paid to the lord of the manor in money, or in kind or by way of services. There could be an entry charge at the start of the tenancy and death duties. The liability was much greater than Freeholders. Copyhold could not change hands without the consent of the Lord of the Manor. Licence was required from the Lord of the Manor to do such things as building houses and cutting down trees.

    B. By the 1500s conventional leases became more common because they were considered more lucrative.

    C. With all leaseholds after the civil war in 1660 there was no longer any requirement for service or military provision. Only rent payments in money or in kind applied.

6. Feoffment became the method of recording sales of land. This was done on site with witnesses. This became a deed transaction by 1400s. There were a number of different documents used to cover what we now regard as conveyancing. Bargain and sale transactions started in the 1400s and superseded or were used as an alternative to feoffment. By 1536 the law tried to force all transactions to be enrolled to prevent secrecy and increase taxation. This was largely unsuccessful due to procedures being evolved to circumvent enrolment.

7. Trusts started with people going on crusades or entering the church and taking vows of poverty. Transferring ownership to a person you trust causes a split between what is called the legal estate (the name the land is in) and the equitable estate (the person/s entitled to it). By the 1700s trusts were commonly created to hold land for the benefit of others. They could avoid taxes. They could as we have seen with our two farms involve a multitude of parties with complex family arrangements.

8. In the 1700s deeds were prepared with as many parts as there were parties. They were cut from one sheet of parchment with wavy lines at the top. One set of wavy lines should match the next when cut.

9. I have not considered any stamp duty issues. These do not impact on the purposes of the deeds.

10. Since the 1800s there has been considerable development in dismantling the privileges of the landed aristocracy. The feudal system did not completely end until 1926.

FREEHOLDS

1. Freeholds were not as we consider them today involving an absolute ownership. Freeholders in the 1700s were still tenants.

2. The original concept was that a Freeholder would as well as paying rent that might be a nominal sum be liable to provide a service that a freeman would not find derogatory to perform. A good example is sending your son off as a knight to fight in the crusades. This was a unpaid service to your overlord. The need to fight was replaced by a tax called Scuttage. For example in Little Baddow in 1086 we have Germond of Oakley as tenant of Ralph Barnard Sherrif of Essex. Ralph Barnard pays the king in relation to his various properties three knights fees. This covers not only the cost of a professional soldier but also his groom, horses and armour. The reference to Fee is the start of the term Fee Simple now found in many deeds of property.

3. So far as our Four French Men were concerned they were in a fairly independent position. They had no liability to Scuttage and their rent was nominal. They probably had to make a payment to the Lord of the Manor when the property changed hands depending on local custom.

4. By the 1300s 50% of England was Freehold. I think it was a lesser percentage in Little Baddow.

5. There were lots of ways lawyers recorded the legal transfer of Freehold land. I will confine myself to those relevant to the documents the subject of this report.

USES AND STATUTE OF USES 1536

1. Many of the documents you will read will have phrases like 'To use and behoof' (old word for benefit). This covers a benefit, advantage or profit in land such as rent.

2. Some understanding of the common law prior to 1536 is required. You have a use whereby A the owner transfers land to B a nominee who in turn holds for A the owner or C a different person. B has the legal estate and A/C have an equitable estate. It was under feudal rules B who had the legal estate that paid the tax. This led to creation of a chain of uses in the nature of a trust. Land that passed by will to an heir was taxed. Landowners created a use to enable someone other than the heir to own the land to avoid tax. (There is nothing new on trying to avoid inheritance tax or death duties!) This is the start of entailing. You interfere with the natural path of inheritance before dying by creating a trust.

3. The statute of uses intended to end the practice of creating uses in property by changing equitable estate into an absolute ownership that was taxable. It tried to invalidate all uses that avoided tax.

4. Henry VIII's idea (or was it the idea of his principal minister the wily Thomas Cromwell) of increasing tax led to botched legislation on uses due to opposition by the wealthy landowners. It failed to destroy the equitable estate properly. Henry VIII tried to strengthen his position by a Statute of Enrolment that made it necessary to record all freehold transfers. It also covered bargains and sales of estates on inheritance. The revolt in 1536 called The Pilgrimage of Grace could have been more to do with land transactions than religious issues such as dissolving the monasteries.

5. The Statute was not repealed until 1925 no doubt because circumventing it was a gravy train for lawyers. They devised a system of lease, release and fictious court actions which I will discuss in detail later in this note.

WILLS AND INHERITANCE

1. The common law was based on primogeniture where the eldest son inherited (or if he died then his eldest son) as the presumed heir. Failing that other sons inherited and then daughters.

2. This changed with the Statute of Wills in 1540. Henry VIII completely underestimated the uprising and protest his Statute of Uses and provision for Enrolment had created. He needed do something to appease the landowners.

3. Landowners were then allowed to determine who would inherit their land. They could devise by will to the heir of their choice.

4. We still have relevant parts of this Act today. The will must be in writing, signed by the person making it and properly witnessed.

5. With inheritance it was not until 1925 that daughters were treated equally to sons.

6. The common law presumption was that if the wife died first the husband only got a life interest if they had a child.

7. The common law presumption was that if the husband died first the wife was entitled to a Dower of one third of the estate for life or until remarriage. She also got all jewellery, ornaments and similar items called the widows paraphernalia. Freeholds that were previous the property of the wife were returned to her. While she lived the husband could not sell without her consent.

8. All this was subject local custom and the practice of the ecclesiastical courts which dealt with probate administration.

9. By 1670 statute confirmed that when there was no will the widow received one third and the children or their heirs received the balance. With no children the widow got one half and the balance went to the husband's family.

10. Wills dealt with transfer of Freehold property without further documentation. This was referred to as a devise whereas personal property like goods and chattels were a bequest.

11. Married women could not make wills without the consent of their husband.

ENTAILMENT

1. With a Freehold estate you are free to sell or devise by will or settle property as you choose but land held in fee tail is limited to the lineal descendants of one person.

2. The term entail evolved from a settlement before death into a stricter settlement that could be made by will or deed. The deed was often a settlement on marriage which introduced provision for supporting children as well as widows

3. You might have property passing exclusively to females or males. (I would not mention the idea of a female entailment to Jane Austen and Mrs Bennett.) Male entailment was the predominant provision.

4. Since the 1600s there was always the potential of barring an entail and converting it into an unconditional freehold. There would be a fictious action for recovery.

5. This is a good time to mention the 1689 Bill of Rights that influenced how the Court of Chancery worked. It would dispense equity according to the fairness not as prescribed by strict common law. This allowed beneficiaries to be true owners and could for example justify barring an entail. (LN Recoveries).

MARRIAGE SETTLEMENTS

1. As previously mentioned widows had rights called the Dower and settlements tried put a stop to this practice.

2. In the 1700s settlements normally related to arranged marriages and not marriages of love.

3. You have a conveyance to trustees as nominees for the use of specified beneficiaries. The consideration was the intended marriage and the benefits of the property stayed with the original owner until the marriage.

4. Normally they gave the original owner and then the husband a life interest. With the very wealthy sometimes the wife only got pin money until he died which was then enhanced by his death.

5. There were often capital sums provided for children which could put financial pressure on the settlement to pay.

6. In our case we have in 1735 a settlement in the nature of a dowery for a granddaughter.

7. The settlements were usually for a term of 1000 years. Nowadays this would be regarded as a virtual freehold.

8. It was fairly standard practice that life interests could be assigned.

HUSBANDS, WIVES, MARRIAGE AND WOMEN'S RIGHTS

1. In 1735 boys could marry at 14 and girls at 12. It is not clear but presumably this was with the parent's consent. The concept was that a girl was adult by the time she started to menstruate.

2. You could get engaged at the age of 7. Presumably this was to facilitate arranged marriages where resources such as land and money were an issue.

3. In reality people did not marry until their late teens or early twenties. Girls were often substantially younger than men when they married.

4. In 1735 there were still a number of secret and even bigamous marriages. There was a concept of a common law marriage. This all ended with the Marriage Act of 1753 which remained in force until 1823. This abolished the idea of a common law marriage. Men and women were not adult until the age of 21. They could not marry under that age without the consent of their parents.

5. Under common law women could inherit. Eileen Spring in her book says in the 1700s 42% of inheritance was by women. Woman generally outlived their husbands thus controlling property in their widowhood. Women were in a strong position if they were not married. The culture then of course was to marry. Marriage was fairly essential for the middle and upper classes as those women could not earn their own living.

6. In 1735 the common law doctrine of coverture still applied. The legal existence of the wife merged with the husband. Her rights were mostly subsumed to her husband. Her legal existence was suspended for the period of the marriage. This English concept was considered very odd by many other nations in Europe.

7. The common law gave the wife some protection in that the husband could not convey the freehold without her joining in. There was however scope for him to lease and receive rent without her consent.

8. There was of course the issue of the husband having rights to sex. He might beat his wife by way of correction.

MORTGAGES

1. With thanks to the Nottingham University manuscripts department for much of the information in this section. Mortgages operate in a similar way today.

2. At the time of our 1742 mortgage there were two ways of creating a charge. The first was a mortgage by conveyance some times called a mortgage in fee. You conveyed the property to your lender with a provision for conveyancing it back once the loan was repaid in full.

3. The second was a mortgage by demise by way of a lease generally for 500 to 1000 years. There was a nominal rent usually 5 shillings a year with a proviso for redemption involving a set date and place for repayment plus interest.

4. Repayment ends the lease and this was done by assigning the lease to a nominee of the owner for the remainder of the term. I do not understand the need for this procedure as surely the lease could be ended by release or surrender. Care needs to be taken in considering this procedure because it looks very much like the ordinary assignment of a lease.

5. It is this second type of deed that relates to our 1742 mortgage that was by demise for 999 years at a peppercorn rent.

6. As regards both types of mortgage although repayment was at a specified place and date, usually one year after its creation this does not mean what it says. Unless there was specific wording once this overran there was an assumption the mortgage could continue for the rest of the term.

7. Many properties remained in mortgage for decades subject to interest being paid once or twice a year. The borrower was often unwilling or unable to repay. There was a culture of treating mortgages as an investment with a regular income. Unlike the Southsea Bubble days of speculation it was a relatively safe investment. In the 1700s farming was a low margin and often risky business with yields as little as 2%. You made much more from a mortgage with 5% interest.

   (Nowadays it is not a lot different with some interest only mortgages that are unlikely to be repaid for decades provided the interest is variable and the rate gives a favourable return.)

8. We also need to consider interest rates. In the 1700s they were stable between 4% and 5% despite the periods of social disruption.

9. They used a term called Usury. In the 1700s there was a papal prohibition on Usury that meant it was a sin to charge interest on a money loan. I am sure the landowners of England largely ignored this decree. It may have been a concern to Roman Catholics.

10. Henry VIII continued to upset the church and the landowners so as further appeasement he passed an Act Against Usury in 1545. This fixed a maximum interest rate and anything above that was Usury. This did not apply to Jews who could charge as much as 54% pa.

11. In 1714 there was an Act reducing the interest rate to 5%. The Act Against Usury was not repealed until 1854.

LEASES (Not part of mortgages, settlements or the lease and release procedure)

1. In the 1700s there were two types of lease, conventional and customary.

2. A conventional lease is much as we have today for a fixed period often with farms of 7/14/21 years. Some times they were for lives or lives. For example 99 years would cover three generations.

3. We have evidence that Hammonds and Priest Lands were leased and under leased but we do not have details. I think it is safe to assume they were conventional leases with the underlessees possibly having tenancy agreements from year to year. There were allotments that may have involved a crop share arrangement.

4. I also mention the customary Copyhold tenancy as this was common in Little Baddow as with the rest of the country until the late 1800s. I have evidence for example that this was the type of tenancy for large parts of Holybread Farm Estate and the Estate of which Joyces Farm in Spring Elms Lane was a part.

5. Care must be taken in comparing rents for conventional and customary tenancies . The customary tenancy could be a lot less because copyholders had to pay things like a Heriot by way of death duty to a lord of the manor. Often they took your best animal by way of tax.

QUIT CLAIM

1. A document used to secure a transaction. All people such as relatives or creditors are asked to sign a quit claim. Doing so they waive all their possible rights and promise not to bring legal action.

2. By the 1700s it was often called a release or releases claim.

3. An example is paying a legacy or annuity by mortgaging land. The recipient of the money signs a quit claim waiving rights against the land out of which the money was raise by mortgage.

COURT OF COMMON PLEAS

1. There are in1735 still various courts dealing with different types of cases. For example some family disputes would be referred to the Court of Chancery to deal with on an equitable basis as to what is fair.

2. The Court of Common Pleas dealt with actions between subject and subject not involving the crown.

3. There was a chief justice supported by two others.

4. This court had exclusive jurisdiction on cases concerning land.

5. One of the problems with court cases in our review period was to ascertain the true cause of action.

6. There was much made of legal fictions as part of collusive litigation. Often this involved facts assumed or even created by the court of for the benefit of the court. There would have been some corruption such as bribing court officials.

ERECTION OF COTTAGES ACT 1588

1. This regulated cottage building. It required each cottage to have a least 4 acres of land and limited the number of people occupying each cottage.

2. There were lots of exemptions and exceptions to this Act. The Act was not repealed until 1775.

3. It may impact on our farms. There are various references in the papers to cottages as well as a farmhouse. I am sure this complied with the acreage requirement. How the limits on occupiers were regulated I have no idea.

WASTE

1. This is nothing to do with sewage or waste ground not being used.
2. This is the concept of doing an act that alters the nature of land for better or worse. The occupier such as a tenant must not do anything to the detriment of the freehold.
3. It is a doctrine that was based in common law and is found in different forms with complex interpretation. Breach makes you liable for damages.
4. For example if you have a life interest in a woodland and cut it down this could be waste even if the land then had a profitable agriculture use. The same applies to knocking down a building and replacing it.
5. Most of the deeds examined by me exclude a liability for waste.

CONVEYANCING PROCEDURES

Gone are the ancient ceremonies of 'delivery of seisin' such as the transfer of a relevant item such as the key to Hammonds Farmhouse or a piece of turf from the Priests Lands to confirm the new freehold owner. We now have fictitious disputes and collusive actions on land in the Court of Common Pleas in Westminster that deals with all property actions. There are two types of action Fines and Recoveries. All actions are started in the Court of Chancery and then transferred to Common Pleas. References to buyer and seller in these notes are just for illustration. These actions were also often used to confirm family gifts. Sometimes manorial courts could deal with things rather than the Court Common Pleas. This system ended in 1833. The whole feudal system did not end until 1926.

Fines

1. The deed of the 2nd August 1764 refers to this procedure.
2. There is an agreement between the parties with an extra copy for the court.
3. With a sale the buyer alleges the seller had agreed to sell and the seller has failed to do so. The seller is in default.
4. For example a father wants to give his farm to his son. Instead of an outright gift the father has to go to court to acknowledge he has already given the farm to his son.
5. There was an out of court settlement called a Final Concord. There were other types of fine action but this was the most common.
6. The matter goes into court where the seller acknowledges they have already given the property to the buyer. An order is made making the buyer the owner of the property.

Recoveries

1. The two deeds of November 1804 refer to this procedure.
2. The buyer brings a case against the seller for recovery claiming he has been unfairly dispossessed from the property by a fictious third party.
3. The seller gets someone to vouch for his title. That person disappears allowing judgement for the buyer. This was popular for getting rid of entails as mentioned in that section of these notes.

4. The procedure was very complex and could involve a series of 3 additional deeds as well as the court action. (More money for the lawyers!) Please refer to Nottingham University manuscripts department for a full explanation.

Lease and Release.
1. Two of the deeds in August 1781 and also the two deeds of November 1804 illustrate this procedure.
2. Common Law allowed a release by one out of possession. For example a landlord holding a reversion to a tenant in possession.
3. During the period 1735 to 1804 this was the most popular format for conveyancing and was used for sales, mortgages and settlements.
4. It avoided enrolment so the transaction was not made public.
5. There were two separate documents intended to be read together.
6. First you had a lease to the buyer as tenant normally for 1 year at a peppercorn rent and for a nominal consideration of 5 shillings.
7. The next day the seller as landlord sold the reversion of the lease to the buyer as tenant giving them the right to the freehold. This swallows up the lease and this is when the real money passed hands.
8. Technically the documents only gave the buyer the rights and interest in the freehold and a court action was required to put the actual freehold title in the name of the buyer.

Index of people

Argent, John 41ff, 54

Austen, Jane 15, 45, 73

Baggott, Annabella 14

Baggott, Richard 14

Balsham, John 12

Barbarous, Joseph 46

Barker, Hannah 27, 42

Barker, William 20, 24, 27f, 42

Barnard, Ralph Sherrif of Essex 72

Barrington, Family 14

Barrington, Sir Francis 13

Barrington, Sir Gobert 50

Barrington, Lord 17, 50

Bartlett, Mr 58

Bennett, Mrs 45, 73

Bocher, John 13

Boultwood, Samuel 58

Bridges, Sir Brook William 14f, 45f, 47f, 50f, 54, 56

Bridges, Frances (Dame Fanny) 15, 45f, 48, 54, 56

Bumpsted, Samuel Lucas 52, 56

Bundock, John (Historian) 4, 46

Butler, Thomas 69

Carter, Bartholomew Churchill 69

Chapman and Andre, Plan 7, 50

Choat, Richard. 65

Clerke, Robert 14

Cromwell, Thomas 72

Darcy, Sir Thomas 13

Davis, Isaac 43

DeGray, William 46

Digby, Elizabeth 47

Digby, Lord Henry 46f

Fitzwalter, Baron 46

Fowler, Christopher 39, 45

Fowler, Edmund 22, 37ff, 45ff

Fowler, Elizabeth 45

Fowler, (family). 42, 46

Fowler, Frances (Fanny) Dame 14f, 45ff

Germond of Oakley. 12, 72

Glanville, John 20, 24, 25, 27, 30, 42

Glascocke, Richard 13

Goodson, Jill (Historian) 4, 37, 46

Gosling, Matthew 42, 43, 48, 51, 54

Grene, Family 13

Grene, Robert 13

Grey, Lord 35

Gyford, Janet (Historian) 69

Hales, Sir Thomas Pym 46f

Harrey, Sarah 41

Hutson, George Junior (Map Maker) 51

Hammond, John 12

Hammond, Thomas 12

Hamonde, Edmund 12

Hart, Ann 53

Hart, Demaris 53

Hart, Elizabeth 53, 62

Hart, Evan 53, 58, 65, 68ff

Hart, Mary. 53, 58, 63, 65ff, 68f

Hart, Noah 53

Hart, Samuel (various generations) 53, 58, 61f, 65

Hart, Sarah 53, 62

Hart, William (various generations) 43f, 48, 50f, 52, 53, 54ff, 58ff, 65, 68

Harvey, Sarah 41

Henry the Eighth 72f, 75

Herward, John 13

Hunt, H G (Historian) 16

Jefferies, John 14

Jones, Evan 58

Jones, Mary 58

Kether, Nathaniel 43

Keys, Gamaliel and son 8, 42, 48, 50f, 54f

Keys, John 8, 42f, 48, 51, 54f

Keys, Hannah 15, 42, 48, 54

Keys, Mr and Mrs 8, 42ff, 55, 57

Knight, Edward Austen 45

Knight, Rev George 45

Knipe, Thomas 43

Leaver, Jim (Historian) 12

Lince, Phyliss 65

Long, Samuel 35, 40

Martin, Robert 17, 20, 24, 43

Merrish & Co (Bank). 60

Mildmay family. 17

Mildmay, Frances. 39, 45

Mildmay, Colonel Henry 13, 14, 22, 45

Mildmay, Sir Henry 13, 17

Mildmay, Sir William 46f

Monk, Nicholas 28, 35, 37, 45

Nicholls, Damaris 58

Nicholls (or Nichols), Family 37

Nicholls, John/Joseph 53, 58

Nicholls, Mr 53, 58

Nicholls, Samuel 53, 58

Nicholls, Susanna. 53, 58

Nicholls, William 53, 58

Nicholson, Family (formerly Nicholls) 37, 46f

Nicholson, Mary 46f

Nicholson, William 37ff, 45, 48

Ougham, James 19

Patteshall, Elizabeth 39, 46

Penninge, Henry 13

Peers, John 19

Perkins, Francis (otherwise Frances) 14

Pledger, Elias 55

Pledger, Family 15

Pledger, Jeremiah 13, 65f, 68f

Reed, William 62f

Rowley, Sheila (Historian) 13f, 17

Rudd, Matthew 13

Sadd, John 40ff, 50, 54

Sadd, John Tagell 40f

Sadd, John & Sons 40f

Sadd, Mr and Mrs 15, 40, 54-56, 57

Sadd, Sarah. 15, 40, 54, 56

Sewell, William 43

Skingly, Mr 32, 35

Smith, John 13

Spring, Eileen (Historian) 74

Stawell, Lord 14

Stoakes (Stokes), Mr 17, 26

Stoakes, Benjamin 19, 24, 26, 28, 35, 45

Stoakes, Sarah 14, 17, 19f, 22, 24f, 27, 28, 30, 35, 40, 56

Stock, James 58

Tagell, Hannah and junior 17, 26, 40, 51, 55

Tagell, John 17, 19f, 24f, 26, 30, 40f, 42f

Tagell, Sarah and junior. 6, 26, 28, 30, 32, 35, 37f, 40, 42f, 45

Tagell, William 14, 17, 19, 25, 26, 28, 29ff, 33ff, 37, 38, 39, 40, 442f

Thompson, Mel (Historian) 12f, 19, 55

Tuffnell, John Jolliffe 46f, 56

Walker, John 13

Waterson, Edmund 45

Waterson, Elizabeth 22, 39, 45f

William, The Conqueror 71

Wolvett, Mr 17, 26

Wolvett, George 19, 25, 26, 30, 35

Wolvett, Sarah 14f, 17, 19, 22, 26, 27, 35, 42

Young, Arthur (Historian) 15

...

Printed in Great Britain
by Amazon